MIAN XIANG 面相

DISCOVER
FACE
READING

Mian Xiang - Discover Face Reading

The author can be reached at:

Mastery Academy of Chinese Metaphysics Sdn. Bhd. (611143-A)
19-3, The Boulevard, Mid Valley City,
59200 Kuala Lumpur, Malaysia.
Tel   : +603-2284 8080
Fax   : +603-2284 1218
Email   : info@masteryacademy.com
Website : www.masteryacademy.com

DISCLAIMER:

Published by JY Books Sdn. Bhd. (659134-T)

INDEX

PREFACE

My introduction to Face Reading came many years ago, as a very young student of Chinese Metaphysics, when I happened to catch a well-known Master on television in Hong Kong.

On the program, this Master conducted a live demonstration of his Face Reading skills before a very sceptical audience and television presenter. He was challenged every step of the way but at the end of the program, the live demonstration had silenced all the critics.

I was absolutely enthralled and that moment was the beginning of my journey into the fascinating science of Mian Xiang or Face Reading. I bought every Chinese book on the subject and set out to study and learn all I could about Face Reading. And I didn't just want to learn it, I wanted to master the art. So I got hold of all the classical literature and visited many masters to help me crack the code in the classics.

I have been fortunate, in recent years, to meet the Master who spurred my interest in Mian Xiang and our conversations have given me much opportunity to exchange ideas and thoughts on Mian Xiang with him and of course, to deepen my knowledge of the subject.

Mian Xiang has helped me in my personal quest of deepening my knowledge of Chinese Metaphysics, particularly in studies like Classical Feng Shui and Astrology over the years as well. This is a field, unfortunately, that is replete with many Grand Masters, Masters and Practitioners, who make many claims. Finding someone who not only has the substance, abilities and teaching skills has not been easy, and having knowledge of Mian Xiang has been essential in helping me separate the proverbial wheat from the chaff.

One part of the motivation behind this book has been the incredible response from my students and members of the public who have attended my Mian Xiang seminars. Students come in solemn and serious to the classes and end up having such a good time and enjoying themselves so much, they are often reluctant to stop for coffee breaks! The public as well has been extremely interested and fascinated in this subject and I have had many requests for a Face Reading book since I began covering Mian Xiang in my public talks.

Undeniably, Mian Xiang is a superb way to gain a gentle entertaining introduction to the extensive field of Chinese Metaphysics which encompasses not just Face Reading, but body-language, palmistry, Chinese Astrology and of course, Feng Shui. After all, everyone has a face and most people, consciously and unconsciously, engage in judgement by face-reading more than they realise.

This book should serve as an invaluable companion to my specially produced DVD series on Mian Xiang, particularly for those who are more inclined to learning via audio-visual forms.

Of course, this book cannot replace the experience that comes from taking one of my seminars but I hope that it will serve to pique and excite your interest in this incredible ancient science. I have made great efforts to ensure it is written in an easy readable style so that with a little imagination, it will hopefully seem like being in a real class with me.

A quick word of advice: Face Reading is not for you to prejudge a person. Understanding a person's characteristics is not the same as judging them. Face Reading is about helping us understand a person, not about categorising him or her as 'good' or 'bad' in that sense. Of course, there are always general principles that we use in Chinese Metaphysics but that does not mean, you should generalise or discriminate against anyone. There are always exceptions to every rule and a good side to every person.

For those of you who are new to the field of Chinese Metaphysics, I hope this book will open a new door to you and afford you with an opportunity to see how lively and fun the field of Chinese Metaphysics can be. The key to Face Reading is not to adopt a stuffy approach but to have fun and practice the techniques on your friends, family and even people you don't know! Pretty soon, your eyes will sharpen and you'll start seeing things in faces you never paid attention to in the past. This is a beginner's text and so is not exhaustive on all the techniques of Face Reading but, by the end of this book, you should be able to actually read a person's face for certain personality traits and of course, that person's luck and fortune.

Enjoy.

Warmest Regards,

Joey Yap
July 29, 2005

Author's personal website :
www.joeyyap.com

Academy websites :
www.masteryacademy.com I www.maelearning.com I www.baziprofiling.com

Joey Yap on Facebook :
www.facebook.com/joeyyapFB

MASTERY ACADEMY
OF CHINESE METAPHYSICS™

At www.masteryacademy.com, you will find some useful tools to ascertain key information about the Feng Shui of a property or for study of Astrology.

To learn more about your personal Destiny, you can use the Joey Yap BaZi Ming Pan Calculator to plot your Four Pillars of Destiny – you just need to have your date of birth (day, month, year) and time of birth. The Joey Yap Flying Star Calculator can be utilised to plot your home or office Flying Star chart. To find out your personal best directions, use the 8 Mansions Calculator.

For more information about BaZi, Xuan Kong or Flying Star Feng Shui, or if you wish to learn more about these subjects with Joey Yap, logon to the Mastery Academy of Chinese Metaphysics website at **www.masteryacademy.com.**

Chapter One:
The Face Never Lies
-The Power of Mian Xiang

There is an old English saying, 'Never judge a book by its cover', which implies that we should never judge people by their appearances. Yet, we are constantly told that appearances matter. The truth is that we judge people based on their faces all the time. Their look. Their appearance. Their face.

He looks like a scumbag.

She looks like a scheming person.

He looks kind-hearted.

He looks like a nice person.

We say these things about people we meet all the time. Yet almost all the time, we are judging someone on an uninformed basis. Now this is not a good practice. It is like judging a person's luck based on the year of the birth and his or her animal zodiac. Hundreds of thousands of people are born in the year of the Dragon – they are not all fierce, ambitious and breathe fire. Similarly, someone who we think looks like a scumbag might turn out to be someone really nice!

That is not to say that you cannot judge a person based on his or her face. You can, as long as you know what you are looking for and what you are looking at! An informed judgment can tell you a great deal about a person. We can certainly find out a lot about them from their appearance – their character, nature, good and bad personality traits, destiny, fortune and/or just their luck for the day – all by looking at their appearance, their face.

That is what Mian Xiang or Face Reading is all about. Mian, which is Face and Xiang, which is Physiognomy or Appearance, is also known as the Chinese Art of Face Reading.

It has a long and illustrious history as a science, having been developed since the time of Huang Di or the Yellow Emperor (2700BC – 2150BC). It is an art born out of the observation

of the physical appearance of a person – shapes, lines, bone structure, features and even Qi colour of the face. At a high level of practice, movements, speech, gestures and little facial tics or expressions can be used to interpret a person's character and nature. Much of the information and techniques in Mian Xiang are drawn from ancient classics like Shen Xiang Quan Pian (神相全篇),

Shen Xiang Tie Guan Dao (神相鐵關刀), Ma Yi (麻夷) and Liu Zhuang (柳庄) which outline the techniques and principles of this immensely accurate science.

During the days of the Imperial Dynasty, Face Reading was one of the sciences deployed by Chinese strategists and Imperial advisors in their role of providing guidance and strategic advice to the Emperors whom they served. For example, whenever an Emperor went off to meet a rival King or perhaps, had a foreign visitor or dignitary come to his court, his Imperial strategist would, using his Mian Xiang skills, be able to immediately size up this person and provide the Emperor with detailed insight and knowledge on the person, enabling the Emperor to determine what to say or not say to that person.

Face Reading was also developed for the purposes of determining suitable candidates for Imperial positions. You see, because of under-developed bureaucratic and administrative structures, it was common for people to have inaccurate birth records or even not really know when they were born. This was especially the case if a person was born during a conflict or warring time, when chaos prevailed and proper time and dates of birth were not kept. The ability of the Chinese Astrologer to accurately forecast such a person's character, nature and Destiny would be difficult.

In the old days, you didn't have to submit your CV to get a job as an Imperial Magistrate; you submitted your BaZi (八字), or your Astrology chart. Face Reading was developed as a means to enable Imperial Mandarins to ensure that candidates for Imperial positions did not secure their positions by using faked dates of birth to exaggerate their Destiny and thus, gave themselves abilities or talents that they did not actually possess.

Face Reading was also employed by mother-in-laws to ensure that their sons married wives who brought luck to the family and not bad fortune. Similarly, mother-in-laws would use it to scrutinize prospective son-in-laws to ensure they were truly wealthy (not just saying they were wealthy!) and would be able to take good care of their daughters.

An astrology chart can be wrong, a CV can be faked, a person can say anything, but the Face does not lie.

What is Face Reading?

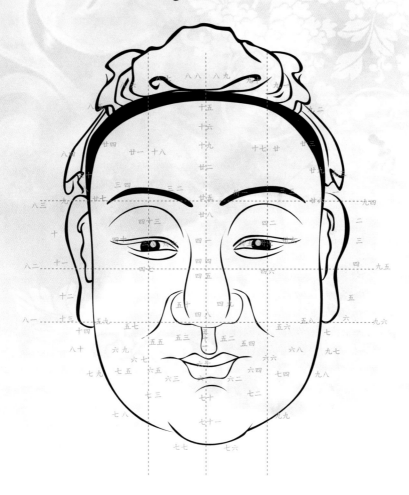

Face Reading is a form of 'Physiognomy' which is one of the Chinese Five Arts (Wu Shu 五術). The term 'physiognomy' refers to the observation of appearances. Physiognomy or 'Xiang' spans not just the observation of the face, but also the palms, body, voice and physical movements. Face Reading or Mian Xiang (Mian being Face) is the most popular method of observation perhaps because it is relatively easy to observe a person's face.

Mian Xiang encompasses techniques of assessing not only facial features, but also facial expressions and 'small' and subtle movements or tics. The twinkling of the eye, the way a person grins, gazes and smiles, or the way he or she speaks, all tell us something about that person.

It is not only the Chinese who sought to develop the science of Face Reading. In ancient Greece, Hippocrates was amongst those who sought to develop the science of Face Reading. Aristotle, in his books, discusses methods of evaluating a person's character from his face.

The difference between Chinese and Western Face Reading is that Chinese Face Reading goes beyond personality traits and character; it focuses on destiny and fortune as well. Chinese Face Reading looks to find out not just the person's personality and character, but also his or her fortune, luck, and talents. Mian Xiang doesn't just tell us if a person is stubborn or not, but whether he or she will enjoy good or bad luck in life, a good marriage or a bad marriage and even, what kind of career he or she should pursue. It is not only an extremely sophisticated science but also a most revealing one.

The face is essentially a map of a person's destiny, fortune and luck. On the face are 100 points, or positions, which govern a person's fortune and luck from the age of 1-100. But there also certain sectors of the face, known as the Officers and the Palaces, which when evaluated, tell us about a person's character, nature, challenges, obstacles, talents and indeed, potential for achievement, his or her destiny. Each region of the face – Upper Region, Middle Region, Lower Region - also governs a different period of a person's life.

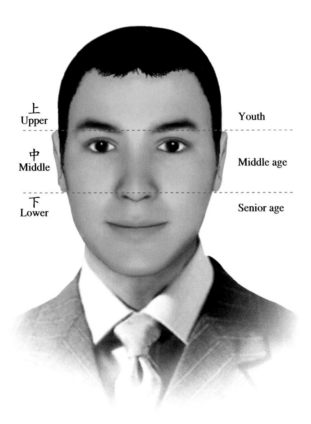

Destiny and the Face

Destiny has been the subject of much study by Chinese sages since the dawn of time. It is from this interest in the science of Destiny that has given rise to the field in Chinese Metaphysics known as the study of Ming 命 (Destiny), one of the Chinese Five Arts (Wu Shu 五術).

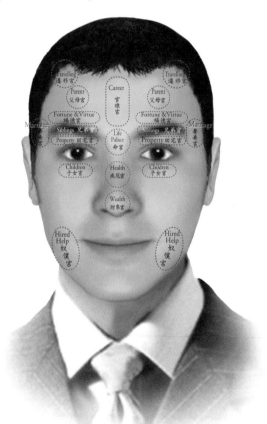

People are fascinated, yet repelled by the notion of Destiny. Who does not want to know what the future holds in store for them? Yet there are those who also think that the concept of Destiny is restrictive, suggesting that human beings have limits when we live in an age of anything is possible, as long as you want it enough.

面相

In my book on BaZi the Destiny Code, I wrote about why knowing and understanding one's Destiny is not just important, but empowering to a person. Simply, it is the path to better decisions, better understanding of yourself and those around you, and in turn, better living.

Now, you might be wondering, what exactly is this 'Destiny' that Joey is talking about?

Another way to think of Destiny is as 'capacity.' Every person in this world is born with a certain capacity – this capacity encompasses the people you will meet along the way, the relationships you will have, the things you can do, your achievements, your talents and your dreams. You can think of it as a life path or life map.

By understanding the path ahead and what is coming, we have the ability to make the right decisions. It is empowerment in the strict sense of the word. Hence, BaZi (Destiny Code or Four Pillars of Destiny) is not just about telling us whether or not we will have a good life and whether or not we will be rich (which is usually what most people are interested in) but is a strategy tool for managing our lives. If you know the path ahead is bumpy, you will brace for the ride. If you know opportunity is lurking ahead, you work harder, push yourself harder and make the most of that window.

BaZi analysis gives a person tremendous empowerment.

It is for these reasons that many top business tycoons (and showbiz personalities) make use of BaZi masters and Feng Shui masters. BaZi is used in top Asian business corporations to help these conglomerates do everything from picking the best date for signing a contract, to placing the right people in the correct positions and to manage suitable businesses. By utilizing BaZi, a conglomerate ensures that they not only have the most capable manager or CEO running the company, but one who's luck also favours the endeavours of the company.

So how then does Face Reading come into the picture?

Speed and time are of the essence in the business world today. Sometimes, decisions have to be made on the split-second. And there isn't the luxury of plotting a BaZi destiny chart for analysis. It is not often that easy to ask for someone's date and time of birth especially if you are meeting them for the first time. Like the stock market, we live in an age of 'right now' forecasting. People want immediate or quick answers.

Face Reading affords BaZi and Feng Shui practitioners the ability to instantly discern a person's fortune or destiny by merely looking at the face. If you intend to go into a partnership with someone, unless they need you, asking them for their date of birth and time of birth to plot a BaZi chart may not be possible. If you are not all that familiar with the person in question, it may be even more awkward.

Face Reading's most powerful advantage is subtlety. Very few people conduct a conversation without looking at the person in the face. In fact, we usually tend to be suspicious of people who don't look us in the eye when they talk to us. So, Face Reading can be subtly employed in the course of business transactions or business meetings to size up a person's character, innate nature and even their potential while you are shaking their hand and saying 'how do you do?'!

Face Reading is even more relevant I think because of the way work and society has developed. It's not just businessmen and tycoons who need to make important decisions, but housewives and average people. It is not just high powered multimillion dollar deals that require inside information, but simple daily transactions like hiring a maid or a bodyguard or babysitter.

Mian Xiang and BaZi:
Later Heaven & Early Heaven.

Many BaZi practitioners often use Mian Xiang as a back-up for their BaZi consultations. Sometimes, it is helpful to confirm certain information about a person's Destiny Chart by examining the face. This is particularly the case when the birth data is uncertain.

However, there are some important differences between BaZi and Mian Xiang which must be understood at this point. In BaZi, we are concerned with the luck that the person is born with or given by Heaven. Your BaZi is your Destiny Code and it determines the capacity that you have in life – how far you will go, what are you talents, how rich you will be, what kind of marriage you will have, what are the pitfalls and the opportunities you will have.

While there is a dynamic element to the BaZi, in the form of the 10 year luck pillars and the Annual Luck pillars, the luck pillars cycle can only improve or enhance the BaZi chart to a certain degree. Your BaZi chart does not evolve. It's pretty much fixed at the moment of your birth.

The face however is not fixed in its appearance. In Face Reading, there is a saying, Xiang You Xin Sheng (相由心生). Your facial features come from your heart.

Of course, this does not mean that overnight, you can become Cindy Crawford. First, because the evolution of your face is gradual and subtle and secondly, because while your face can change, certain aspects of the face (bone structure for example) will not change substantially.

Those of you who have read my book, the BaZi – The Destiny Code, no doubt will be wondering, wait a minute, isn't Destiny already outlined since the date and time of our birth by the Heavenly powers?

Yes, but Destiny also has two aspects: Early Heaven Destiny (Xian Tian Ming 先天命) and Later Heaven Destiny (Hou Tian Ming 後天命). Early Heaven Destiny is the part outlined by your birth date and your BaZi chart. This is the part that you cannot change substantially – you can only chose to avoid certain outcomes where possible or moderate the impact of certain problems.

Later Heaven Destiny relates to your current deeds, actions or lack of action and is reflected in your face and your palms. What you chose to do, or not do, and the outcome of your actions, is reflected in your face. Accordingly, facial features can be changed, if the person chooses to change his or her actions or attitude. Of course, what you can change is limited to the boundaries of your Early Heaven Destiny but there certainly are things within your Destiny, that are within you and your heart, to change. Hence, good fortune comes from the heart. Change the way you think or behave, and your face and accordingly your fortune, can change as well.

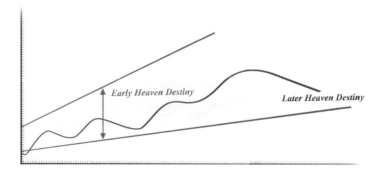

Face Reading - Astrology - Feng Shui: Which Is What?

Mian Xiang (Face Reading), BaZi (Chinese Astrology) and Feng Shui are different fields of studies within the broad field of Chinese Metaphysics. Though they are different fields, they complement each other.

BaZi, which is a form of Chinese Astrology, helps us identify, plot and decode our Destiny through our birth data, the date and time of our birth. A good Feng Shui practitioner will always check a person's BaZi before implementing any Feng Shui solutions or changes.

Mian Xiang enables Feng Shui and BaZi practitioners to see aspects of a person's Destiny that we might not immediately spot in that person's BaZi by observing the facial features or enable practitioners to make

a quick evaluation of the person's problem if for some reason, that person's BaZi information is not available. For instance, the moment we spot a knot on the bridge of the nose, dark patches on the corners of eye and sunken temples, we immediately know that the person has potential "relationship problems".

BaZi and Mian Xiang enable the diagnosis of the person's problem, before the implementation of the prescription, through Feng Shui. Through BaZi and Mian Xiang, we find out what the problems, obstacles or difficulties of the person are, and then we utilize Feng Shui to help solve the problems or minimize their effects.

Why Learn to Read Faces?

Well, it is a skill that is not only invaluable but useful. It gives us a definite edge in our everyday lives when we have to meet and deal with people from all walks of life. Besides, it certainly makes for interesting conversation over dinner, although you may want to stick to just telling people about the good things, not the bad points on the faces.

We often instinctively rely on first impressions to judge people more seriously, size up people or just form a conclusion. And we often have to make such judgments because there is no other way of judging the person. Anybody who has had to pick a maid knows that biodatas are not often helpful (as much of the information could be manufactured) and he or she often ends up making a judgment based on a photograph. At a higher level, university degrees, CVs and qualifications may also not be reflective of the person's qualities (as these days a degree or a CV can also be made-up or exaggerated) and again, we have to rely on our gut feel or just what the person looks like.

It is handy to have a back up skill when it comes to making decisions, be it a decision of whether or not to date someone, whether or not to hire someone, or whether or not to close a million dollar deal with someone. It is in these circumstances that face reading is very useful. With face reading, you can make informed decisions on a person, be more confident in your dealings with people and even tell if a person is telling you the truth or a big fat whopping lie.

Even when the information is accurate and verified through those sophisticated personality tests or a grueling interview, a person's CV won't tell you, for example, if he or she has loose lips. And in the corporate world, we all know the famous saying, loose lips sink ships. If you are involved in a business that requires confidentiality or at least someone who will not blurt out important information, looking at the person's CV will not tell you if he or she can be discreet or not. How do you make sure your accountant is someone who will not divulge any details of your business? Here's a clue – don't hire someone who has a horse smile, as in, his or her gums can be seen when he or she smiles. Especially do not hire him or her if he or she also has big eyes since this person is likely to be gullible, far too friendly and prone to blabbing information out at the wrong times!

Most importantly, tests or profiling techniques will certainly not tell you whether or not a person is going through good luck or bad luck. Why is it important to know whether or not a person is going through good or bad luck? Well, simply put, if you hire an employee going through bad luck for a particular year or stage of his or her life or perhaps facing some legal or relationship problems, it may just be that it is you, the employer, who is affected by that bad luck or stuck with that person's problems! By examining a prospective candidate's face, you will be able to discern if it is a good idea to hire the person this year or perhaps, it is wiser to wait one year, before deciding to bring that person into your organization.

In the following chapters I will introduce you to the fundamental concepts of Mian Xiang, such as the 100 year map of the face and the twelve palaces of the face, and also explaining how different features of the face can be used to read not just a person's fortune and destiny, but character traits and personality features. Some knowledge of the Ba Gua and the Heavenly Stems and Earthly Branches is helpful but I have deliberately avoided as much 'technical' terms as possible and concentrated hard on ensuring this book is accessible, easy to read and most importantly, an entertaining, beginner's book!

Face Reading – An Inborn Human Nature

Face reading is really not as difficult as you might think because really, most of us already subtly practice some form of face reading. Most of us can tell, for example, when someone is happy or sad, or in a bad mood or in high spirits, because we can see it in his or her face. Mian Xiang is a science that essentially studies these features or details on a face, categorises them and creates recognition criteria, and of course, provides memorable names.

Remember, instinctively we are all face readers and we all practice face reading in our daily life, simply in a less informed manner. Once you have got to the end of this book, you will be doing so in an informed manner, with accurate conclusions. Face Reading encompasses many common sense techniques and once you understand the logic behind the system, you will be able to learn and pick up the techniques very quickly.

A few tips on picking up Face Reading: firstly, practice on a daily basis. You have to keep at it and persist with what you have learnt. Read anyone and everyone's face, even the people you don't know! You'll be amazed how quickly you remember and recall what you have learnt. Secondly, try as hard as possible to learn and commit to memory the 100 year map of the face. This will be extremely helpful when it comes to practicing Face Reading.

Of course, a word of caution also. Face Reading must be practiced in an unbiased way and without prejudice – it is immensely useful in business but it shouldn't rule your life. Just because someone's facial features tell you that he has certain, undesirable or unpleasant characteristics, this should not be the reason for you to sever your friendship with him. You may avoid doing business with him, or you may decide not to hire him to work for you but there's no reason to go overboard and become paranoid or suspicious of all the people around you.

And remember to have a lot of FUN. Face Reading is a lively art - share and practice it with your friends and have fun (and prepare for a good time!)

Chapter Two:
The Essentials of Face Reading

An important starting point in Face Reading is learning to recognise face shapes. Face shapes are a good starting point for Face Reading because most people can tell one shape from another quite easily and obviously. It is a gentle introduction to the art of training your eyes to discern different, sometimes subtle, differences in facial features. Face shapes also enable you to undertake basic or general readings about the person.

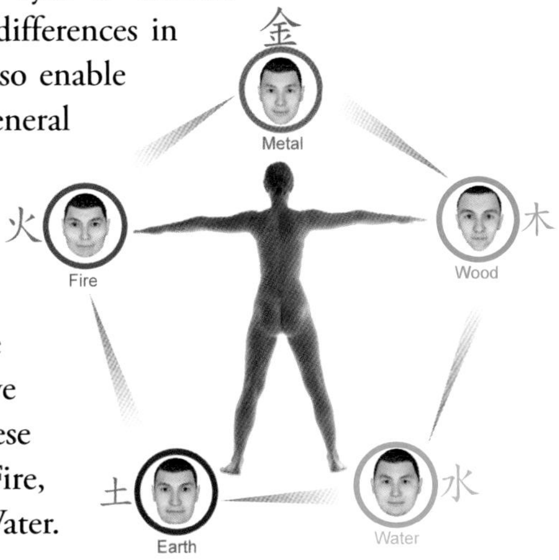

金
Metal

火
Fire

木
Wood

A common core that runs through all of the Chinese Five Arts is the use of the Five Elements and the Five Element cycles. What are these Five Elements? They are Fire, Earth, Metal, Wood and Water.

土
Earth

水
Water

Face reading is considered a form of Physiognomy, which is one of the Chinese Five Arts (Wu Shu 五術). Hence, Face Reading also makes use of the Five Elements as part of its key basic principles. The five basic shapes of the face are one way in which the Five Element principle is utilized in face reading – the five basic face shapes are derived from the Five Elements.

The Five Elements do not just provide us with five basic face shapes, but they also enable us to gain a more sophisticated reading of a person's face, through understanding which features on the face relate to the Five Elements and how those facial features interact, based on the Five Element cycles.

Often, to obtain a clearer and more sophisticated reading, not only is the face shape or facial features observed, but Face Reading practitioners overlay the Five Element theory onto the face and determine how the inter-relationship between the Five Elements impacts on our observations and readings. For example, when we look at a Fire shaped face, we must also observe the eyebrows, eyes and forehead to see if these qualify the Fire shaped face. We also need to look at the Mouth, which represents Water, to see if it impacts on the Fire shaped face.

Yes, one feature or one aspect of the face, such as the shape, can be read in isolation but to form a clear and more precise conclusion about a person's fortune or an aspect of his or her life, we have to look at several parts of the face, a technique in Face Reading known as Hun Liu Fa (混流法) or Multiple Position Reading.

Hence, a good understanding of the Five Elements, and a little bit of knowledge of the Ba Gua, 10 Heavenly Stems and 12 Earthly Branches is helpful in determining the quality structure of a face. For example, generally, a Wood face should be complimented with Water facial features. Why? This is because Water nourishes Wood in the production cycle of Five Elements. Likewise, if a Wood face has strong Metal features, then this denotes bad fortune because in the theory of the Five Elements, Wood is destroyed by Metal.

Learning The Five Elements (Wu Xing 五行)

The theory of Five Elements or Wu Xing is the backbone of Chinese Metaphysical studies, from medicine to Feng Shui, from BaZi (Destiny) to Face Reading. The Chinese believe that the entire science of the universe can be related to the Five Elements – Metal, Wood, Water, Fire, Earth – and how these forms of energy transform and inter-react.

The word 'elements' is not the most accurate word. Wu Xing in fact relates to Five Phases of Qi. Similarly, the terms "Metal", "Wood", "Water", "Fire" and "Earth" are simply used because they contain attributes that resemble the nature of the Five Phases of Qi.

In the study of the Five Elements, there are three important cycles that must be mastered and understood. They are the production cycle, the control cycle and the destruction cycle. By understanding the nature and order of the Five Elements, we can understand how each feature on the human face interacts with one another. We will know whether if our face is balanced or imbalanced. Other than for aesthetic purposes, balance is the goal of all Chinese Metaphysical studies, including BaZi, Feng Shui and Face Reading. When a face has well-balanced features, a person can be said to have a 'good fortune' face.

Learning the Five Elements is a lot easier if you use your imagination and also think about the way the elements inter-react in real life. You'll find after some time that it all makes simple common sense!

The Production Cycle 生

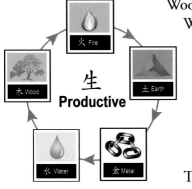

Water nourishes plants: thus Water produces Wood. Wood is used to make Fire; so Wood produces Fire. Fire in turn burns material into ashes and forms Earth. Fire produces Earth. Earth is where we can find minerals. So Earth produces Metal. Metal when condensed will liquefy. Thus Metal produces Water. This process is known as the productive sequence. This cycle is in harmony and in constant movement.

The Weakening Cycle 洩

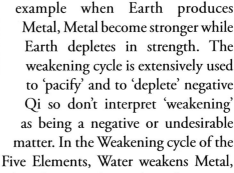

When an element produces another, it is weakened because of the energy needed to produce the other element. For example when Earth produces Metal, Metal become stronger while Earth depletes in strength. The weakening cycle is extensively used to 'pacify' and to 'deplete' negative Qi so don't interpret 'weakening' as being a negative or undesirable matter. In the Weakening cycle of the Five Elements, Water weakens Metal, Metal weakens Earth, Earth weakens Fire, Fire weakens Wood and Wood weakens Water.

The Destruction Cycle 剋

Now, a word of caution: in Chinese Metaphysics, we must remember that certain words like destroy, control or counter, are translations. Do not be focused on whether a cycle is positive or negative, good or bad – it often depends on the circumstance as to whether a Destruction Cycle is good or bad. Sometimes, a Destruction is needed to bring back balance to a situation.

Generally, when the elements destroy, or over control or counter each other, there is imbalance. When the natural order of the Five Elements is altered, there can be disharmony. Water putting out Fire; Fire melting Metal; Metal chopping Wood; Wood (roots of plants) piercing through the Earth; and Earth containing Water are how the Destruction Cycle works.

Now that you have an idea of how the Five Elements work, let's start looking at basic face shapes and their attributes.

The Five Basic Face Shapes

Now, visualisation and imagination are very important in Face Reading. Don't just memorise the face shapes – try to visualise what the Five Elements look like and how they inter-react. Imagine the shapes (what does a piece of Wood look like?) and features (what impression does a hunk of rock give you?) This will help you not only remember the features of the particular face shape, but also help you determine which is the face shape when you engage in practice.

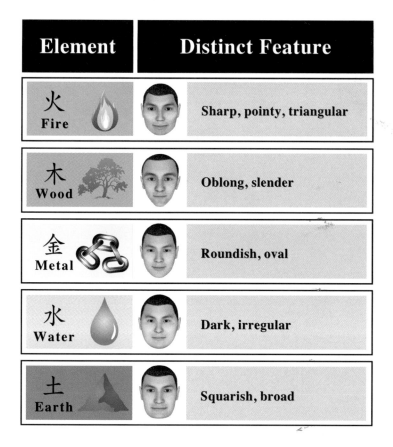

Element	Distinct Feature
火 Fire	Sharp, pointy, triangular
木 Wood	Oblong, slender
金 Metal	Roundish, oval
水 Water	Dark, irregular
土 Earth	Squarish, broad

The Wood Face – The Thinker

Commonly, people with Wood faces have oblong, elongated and thin faces. These faces are also triangular in shape, with a slightly larger forehead and a small chin. People with Wood faces often have corresponding facial features – shapely noses, long ears or long eyebrows. The physical appearance of people with Wood faces is also 'wood-like' – they are usually tall and thin.

Wood Face

In classical texts on Mian Xiang, Wood features indicate a person who is persistent, benevolent, understanding, generous and kind. This is because Wood is the only element in the Five Elements that is always growing. Fire, Water, Metal and Earth do not grow without assistance. Fire for example, needs to be fed Wood to grow.

People with Wood-shaped faces are often people who persevere and who constantly strive to achieve success. Now, think of a tree – it doesn't shoot up several inches suddenly overnight, but grows slowly and steadily. Thus, Wood-shaped faces indicate people who are usually slow and steady, but who win the race.

Normally, Wood-shaped faces indicate individuals who are suited for careers that relate to medicine, research and development, education or social services. This is because in the study of Five Elements, Wood relates to growth. Hence, Wood-shaped faces indicate individuals who can teach, educate or bring about progress. But that doesn't mean people with Wood-shaped faces are only suited for medical research or serving as doctors or teachers. There are a good number of Wood-shaped faces in fields like public service or politicians with Wood-shaped faces. This is because Wood-shaped faces belong to careful thinkers who make good strategists and policy makers.

Now, let's take things to the next level and attempt to be a little more sophisticated with our face reading. Wood, as an element, must be nourished and supported. What nourishes Wood? Water of course.

In the study of Face Reading, and as you will learn as you go through this chapter, the Water star is represented on the face by the mouth. Hence, a person with a Wood-shaped face, who also has a balanced mouth, meaning, upper and lower lip are the same shape and size, is a person who achieves success through perseverance and diligence and that success comes in twos for this person. A Wood-shaped face with a good mouth is a good combination in Mian Xiang.

If a piece of wood is strong and hard, it needs to be made 'useful' through chopping. Thus, a strong Wood face, coupled with Metal features indicates a person who is skilled in financial management, leadership or dynamic qualities that enable the achievement of significant social status. Now, the element of Metal is represented by the Cheeks on the face. Strong Wood faces should have modest sized cheeks – just enough Metal. This indicates a person who is a careful thinker and an excellent decision maker.

If a person with a strong Wood face has very large cheeks, there is too much Metal chopping wood. This denotes that the person often has contradicting behavior, or irrational thinking. Their actions contradict what they say or believe in.

Wood-faced individuals will find that much innovation takes place around Spring time, the prime season of Wood. Projects and endeavours that commence during February, March and April will usually meet with success or good progress. This is because, in the study of the Five Elements, these months are regarded as Wood months and during these months, Wood energy is prosperous.

Wood face with large cheeks

The Water Face – The Entrepreneur

Water has no fixed shape or form – accordingly, individuals with Water faces often have irregular shaped faces. The most common type of Water face is the round or chubby face. The skin is usually dark or tanned. People with a Water-face shape will usually be on the short or petite side and a little plump, or maybe even slightly overweight. Their appearance is fleshy and their bodies are usually meaty. Usually, they have a tummy or hefty stomach, and generous rear ends.

Water Face

Water-faces may not be supermodels, but what they lack in looks, they make up in the ability to adapt to circumstances. Water-faces are survivors, people who can take on financial

和 相

and career challenges, obstacles and difficulties. Like the element of Water, which changes form and shape to fit the container, Water-faced people are highly adaptable and quick-witted. Many Water-faced people are entrepreneurs or businessmen. In the study of the Five Elements, Water relates to wisdom, the ability to make good use of one's knowledge to make good decisions or take the right steps. Hence, Water-faced people are often brainy.

Water-faced people are sometimes viewed as opportunists, people who see a buck in everything or people who thirst for power. Sometimes, they are seen as people without principles when in fact they are simply quick-witted. Water-faced people are often self-driven and usually will achieve financial success at a young age. They may also achieve political success or entrepreneurial success at an early age.

Now, in Face Reading, we must always remember that there are general principles and then there are qualifying principles. A person may have a Water face but the presence of certain facial features will qualify the extent the general principles or characteristics are applicable to the individual. For example, a Water-faced person who has an over-developed mouth or chin (meaning a very large mouth with thin lips or a sharp and protruding chin) usually has a shady character, is most likely a hypocrite and definitely someone with potentially sinister intentions.

What's the reasoning behind this? The mouth and chin are considered Water element in Mian Xiang. Over-developed mouth and chin features, coupled with a Water-face, denotes too much water. That is why the person's character becomes shady and usually cunning.

Overly large mouth on a water face

Fair-skinned Water faces are often people who are witty and highly intelligent and who make decisions quickly and intuitively. Fair-skinned Water faces are equivalent of 'clear water'. Now, obviously, we want water to be clear and clean. When water is clear, the thinking and personality is clear. A dark-skinned Water face is like murky water, their thoughts are deep and often confused.

See how easy it is to understand basic personality nature? Let's continue on with the next element …

The Metal Face – The Officer

Metal element faces are usually the easiest to spot. Metal faces are usually roundish and the bone structure is often defined, making their faces appear strong, sturdy and aggressive. Their faces are not usually bony, but sturdy. Usually, they have oval shaped faces. They also usually have broad chins and foreheads. Metal faces usually have pasty or pale complexions.

Metal Face

In the study of the Five Elements, Metal represents justice, righteousness, altruism, courage, strength and determination. Thus, you will often find Metal-faced people have these characteristics. Other traits of Metal-faced people include courage, a forthright nature and often, they are people who are highly principled. These are people who believe in the law or will fight for what they believe in. Metal-faced people are careful and cautious in their decision-making, often weighing up the pros and cons before taking any action or going one way or another. You won't find Metal-faced people trying to smooth talk their way into or out of any situation, nor are they the mischievous type. Accordingly, Metal-faced people are often suited for jobs in legal or administrative fields. They are natural born leaders and often provide support and strength to those around them.

Metal people can also be quick-tempered and calculative. Now, you might be wondering, how do we arrive at some of these attributes? Remember what I said earlier about the importance of visualizing and thinking in pictures? What happens when you make Metal hot? It stays hot for a long time – hence Metal people can lose their cool easily if they are provoked. But Metal is also the only one of the Five Elements that cuts through objects. Hence, this is the reason why Metal-faced people can be calculative.

While Metal-faced people are normally decisive, if the face is too bony, meaning the bone structure of the face protrudes excessively (Metal faces usually do not reveal bones), or if this person has shaded or hooded eyes, they are likely to be slow-decision makers.

Metal faces that have narrow chins or slanted foreheads are people who will hold personal grudges and who will never ever let you forget anything you have ever done to them, no matter how minor.

Shaded or hooded eyes

The Fire Face – The Entertainer

Fire faces are usually broad in the center of the face (the nose region) and slender on the upper regions (forehead area). Hence, an easy way to identify a Fire face is to look for someone with a narrow or tight forehead and a broad chin. Fire faces belong to people who are usually sturdy looking. They are rarely chubby and usually have defined noses and cheekbones. Fire faces usually have reddish complexions and they usually have striking or charismatic eyes.

Fire Face

In the study of the Five Elements, Fire relates to manners, politeness and beauty. Hence, Fire faces belong to people who value good manners, are always polite and cordial in nature, are elegant in their mannerism and behave well.

This is because Fire in the Five Elements also relates to beauty and a person's sense of 'face value'.

Our eyes are drawn attracted to bright lights and brightness. Hence, Fire faces usually belong to people who work in the entertainment, media, arts or public relations fields.

Fire is also the only element that spreads. Its role is illumination of the darkness. Hence, Fire faced people are usually the sort who like to share their ideas and dreams. These are people who make great motivational speakers, as they are great at influencing and inspiring people.

Now, we always say to children, don't play with Fire because Fire can suddenly flare up. Hence, Fire faced people can be very fierce and short tempered. There is usually a duality to their nature – they can be bold and ambitious, but easily can turn into vicious and angry people.

Fire faced people are adventurous and can often persevere at a task till they achieve what they want. They are usually also very showy people and it is not uncommon to find Fire faced people excelling at sports or dance, anything which involves demonstrating their physique. Fire also represents brilliance so Fire faced people are usually smart, highly attractive or have a magnetic personality. They often possess intelligence and creativity.

While Fire seems bright and burning, it is often 'empty' inside. Hence, Fire faced people, for all their outward positive appearances, often lack confidence in

themselves and sometimes, in others. Finally, Fire flickers. It is never constant in size or shape. Hence, Fire faced people are sometimes fickle. They do not give their trust easily and often like to take matters in their own hands.

Fire Face with protruding mouth

What happens if you see a person with a Fire shaped face and a very distinct or protruding mouth? Remember we said earlier that the mouth belongs to the Water element? Over-developed mouths denote strong Water. If it happens to be on a Fire face, then this denotes an imbalance of the elements. In the study of Mian Xiang, this is called Fire and Water Clashing, indicating that the person has extremist ideas or behaves in an extremist manner.

Large cheeks on Fire Face

On the other hand, a Fire face goes well with large cheek bones. Cheeks represent the Metal element and in this case, a Fire face with prominent cheek bones is called a Fire Forging Metal formation. These faces belong to people with great perseverance and determination.

The Earth Face – Always Practical

The Earth face doesn't need much imagination to figure out. Yes, these are people who have faces that look like a hunk of rock! They have broad or wide faces, with wide mouths, broad noses, wide ears and usually pretty fluffy eyebrows. The face appears to be like a big square. Earth faced people are usually calm and easy going in nature. Don't expect the Earth faces in your group of friends to be the life of the party – chances are, they are the quiet ones in the group. They are usually calm and reserved, even in crisis situations, and usually prefer keeping their thoughts to themselves.

Earth Face

In the study of the Five Elements, Earth is the only element that does not move. Hence, Earth faced people often need a bit of a shove to get going. Normal motivation that gets most people into gear will not work on Earth people. They need very compelling or strong reasons before embarking on their goals. Earth faced people are often also great procrastinators.

Now, this does not mean that Earth faced people are slow or less intelligent. A hunk of rock that just sits there appears to be doing nothing but that doesn't mean nothing is going on. A rock, once it gets moving, will crush anything in its way. Earth faced people, when they set their heart on something, are capable of being scheming, ruthless and a powerful force to be reckoned with. And remember, you need to use dynamite in order to blast your way through rock. Earth faced people make solid opponents and are not to be under-estimated.

Earth in the Five Elements relates to trustworthiness. What do we often find buried in the earth? Treasures. Hence, Earth faced people are generally very trustworthy in nature and make good confidants because they can keep secrets well! The only exception to this rule is a crooked nose on an Earth faced person. In the study of Mian Xiang, a crooked nose is one of the indicators of a sly nature.

Despite their slow and ponderous ways, Earth people are often millionaire material. Their practical, diligent and steady nature means they often are able to accumulate much wealth through hard work. A field that is toiled for the first time may not yield much of a harvest but over the years, the land will eventually yield a bountiful harvest. Their durable nature also gives them long life and generally better health.

Crooked nose on an Earth Face

It's a Rock, It's a Piece of Wood
– Can't Tell the Element?

Okay, we're only on Chapter Two so don't be too worried if you have difficulty identifying facial shapes. Remember, not everyone has the same sense of imagination and some of us take longer than others to learn to discern facial shapes. The trick is to keep practicing and not be disheartened. And let me also share with you a little secret of the trade.

Some faces are made up of TWO elements.

You do not always see people with pure Fire shaped faces or obviously Water shaped faces. Just as human beings are complex in nature, so their faces are often complicated in shape. People often have more than one basic nature or more than one personality characteristic, so don't be surprised that they sometimes have faces that have two dominating elements. More often than not, you should expect to see faces that are a fusion of the five basic shapes.

The trick is to look for the 'dominating element' or dominant feature in the face. Once you have identified that feature, you can easily determine the element type of the face.

What does Face Reading Tell You?

Face Reading is an extremely useful skill that enables you to discern the person's personality just by looking at his or her face. The face is in fact a visual representation of a person's characteristics and personality. How a person handles what life throws at him or her in the form of opportunities or obstacles is determined largely by his or her personality. And how they handle what life throws up, determines their quality of life – how far people can go in life, how much wealth they can amass, and of course, their personal happiness.

When coupled with the 100 year map of the face, which outlines the 100 Year positions, you not only can discern people's personality and character, but also at which points in time, down to the exact year, they will have good or bad fortune. So, the next step is to learn and master the 100 Year Positions on the face.

100 Positions for 100 Years

An important key to unlocking Face Reading is the Chinese 100 year map of the face. This face map marks out 100 positions on the face, with each position corresponding to one year in a person's life.

Now, it is not easy to learn 100 positions on the face. 100 points is a lot to remember, even for someone with an excellent or photographic memory. What I usually do in my Mian Xiang classes is break it down into 5 digestible chunks, which makes it not only easier to learn, but less intimidating for the students.

Usually my students will ask – do we really have to learn every single one of the 100 year positions? Yes and there is a really good reason why you need to know these 100 year positions. Face Reading, like any Chinese Metaphysical practice, requires a point of reference at all times. You need something to start your analysis. Where do you begin to look?

Also, most of the time, when people know you are a student of Face Reading, they will ask you for a 'quickie' reading. How are you going to perform such a reading? That is why the 100 Year Positions is a very useful and an essential reference point. All you have to know is what age the person is, look at the corresponding position on the face, and you can immediately tell if the person is in good luck or bad luck for that year!

Now, I must point out that many of these positions have quaint or sometimes downright strange names in Chinese. I have translated the names and terms into English but don't at any point be misled by the names. They are just terms. If you find them difficult to digest or understand, then stick to the numbers of each position.

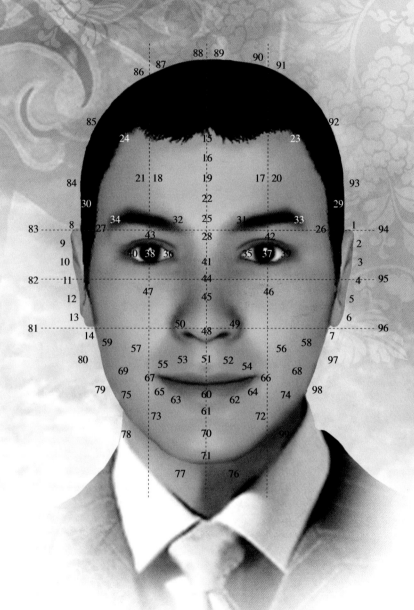

100 Year Map for Males

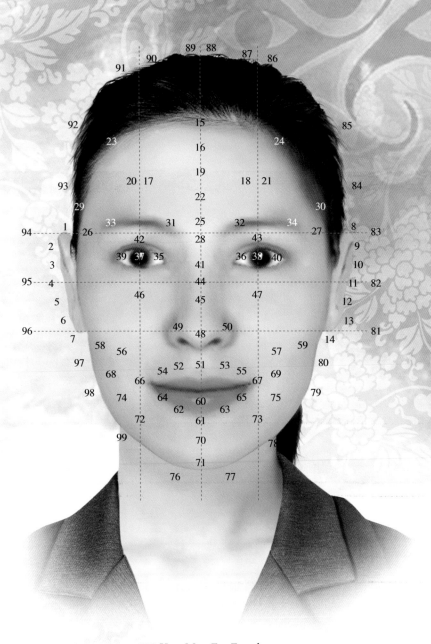

100 Year Map For Females

An important point to remember throughout this book is that the 100 positions are different for males and females. You need to 'flip' the 100 year face map for the females. This means the 100 year map begins on the left side of the face for males, and on the right side of the face for females, with only the central axis numbers (those that run down the center of the nose, from the forehead to the chin) being the same.

Face Reading is a serious Chinese science but I find that when students have fun learning something, not only do they find it easier to remember what they have learnt, but it stays in the mind longer. So, I urge you to go through this section, and all the subsequent chapters, with a nice big mirror on hand. As you read through each of the age positions, try to find it on your own face and observe what is there. You'll soon find you have little difficulty remembering which position is what age!

A Position for Every Year in Your Life

The Chinese regard the 9 months spent in the womb as part of the age calculation. Accordingly, when a person is born, they are regarded as 1 year old. So, remember to add one year to your age when you are looking for the corresponding age position or Xu Ling 虛齡 on the 100 year face map. So for example, if you are currently 28, you need to evaluate the facial feature in position 29 on the 100 year map to determine your luck.

This is a very general section on the 100 year map, designed more to familiarise you with the positions rather than the details. Remember, you need to be able to learn how to walk before you can run. We will delve deeper the meanings of each position in Chapter Three.

Grouping the Positions

One of the fastest and easiest ways to familiarizing yourself with the 100 positions is to group them into common age groups: childhood, youth or adolescence, middle age, senior age and old age. I will go into the details of each and every position in Chapter 3 but to give you a little teaser, I have included some general information about how the different age positions are used in Face Reading here.

Childhood (Ages 1-14)

Remember what I said earlier about how the 100 year map is different for males and females? When you are determining the positions for ages 1-14, remember that you start counting from the left ear for the male and the right ear for the female. So, the left ear represents ages 1-7 for males and the right ear ages 8-14 for males. The right ear represents ages 1-7 for females and the left ear ages 8-14 for females.

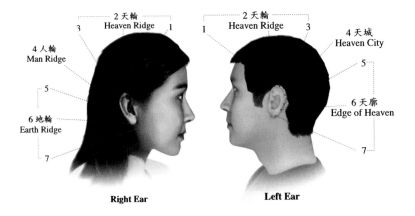

Right Ear   **Left Ear**

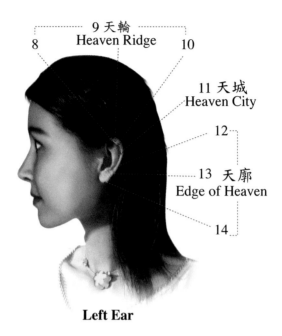

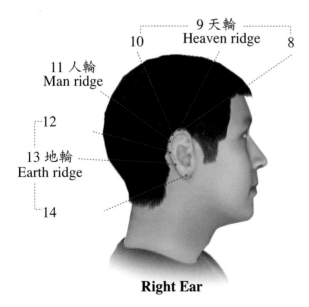

Left Ear

8
9 天輪
Heaven Ridge
10
11 天城
Heaven City
12
13 天廓
Edge of Heaven
14

Right Ear

10
9 天輪
Heaven ridge
8
11 人輪
Man ridge
12
13 地輪
Earth ridge
14

Youth (Ages 15 – 30)

For both males and females, ages 15-30 are located on the forehead region. The area is the same, but some positions are flipped for males and females.

Since the forehead governs a person's luck between the ages of 15-30, we can conclude that a person with a badly formed forehead will have lots of negative luck or challenges and obstacles between the ages of 15-30.

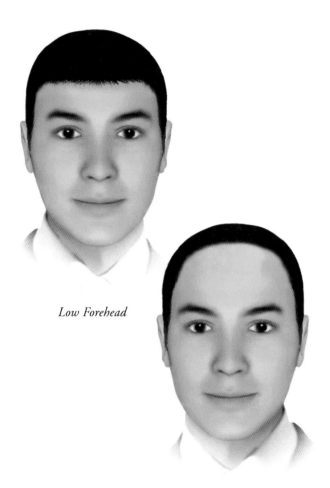

Low Forehead

High Forehead

What is a badly formed forehead you might be wondering? A low-set forehead, a narrow forehead, scarred forehead or a forehead with protruding bumps or lumps is considered a badly formed forehead. Generally, we like foreheads to be smooth (no scars or bumps), tall and broad. People with good foreheads will have success at school or have good careers, from a young age. High foreheads also usually belong to more intelligent people.

Middle Age (Ages 31-50)

The age positions for the ages 31-50 can be separated into two areas: the eyebrows and the eyes, which govern the ages of 31-40 and the nose and the cheeks, which govern the ages of 41-50.

As usual, you need to remember to 'flip' the life map depending on whether it is a male or female reading. For males, the ages 31-34 begin with the left eyebrow and alternate between the left and right eyebrow. For females, begin with the right eyebrow.

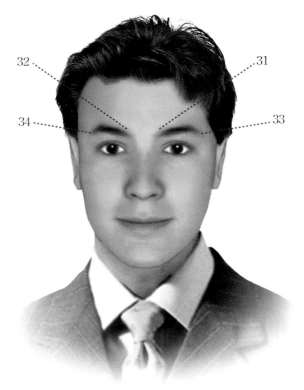

Age 31 - 34 (Male)

The ages of 31-40 are often the ages when most people achieve advancement in life and in their careers. A person's eyebrows will tell us how well they can do between 31-34. Eyebrows that are broken, sparse or too thick denote difficulties during the ages of 31-34, in particular, a person's ability to persevere in challenging times. Weak eyebrows also indicate difficulties in a person's career and that his or her prowess up the corporate ladder will be fraught with challenges. Conversely, an elegant eyebrow, one which is not too thick or too thin, belongs to a person who will enjoy a high flying career and excellent good fortune during ages 31-34.

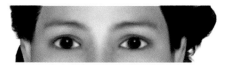

Elegant eyebrows

For the age of 35-40, we need to look at the eyes. Generally, we like eyes to be the same size, as this indicates a stable fortune between the ages of 35-40. Eyes that are different in size indicate fluctuating luck, with career and relationship changes.

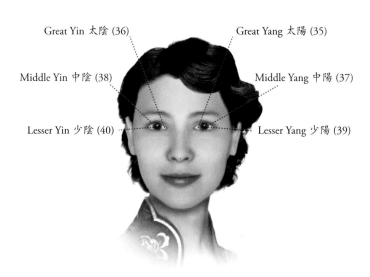

Great Yin 太陰 (36) Great Yang 太陽 (35)

Middle Yin 中陰 (38) Middle Yang 中陽 (37)

Lesser Yin 少陰 (40) Lesser Yang 少陽 (39)

Good eyes are eyes that are lively and have spirit, what we call 'Yan Shen 眼神' in Chinese. Now, do not let the word 'spirit' confuse you – it has nothing to do with ghostly apparitions. If you look in the dictionary, you will find that spirit also refers to vitality and liveliness. It is this 'spirit' that I am talking about. So when we say the eyes have 'spirit', we mean they are alive, alert, sharp and have a lot of charisma. A spirited eye is not dull, lifeless and watery.

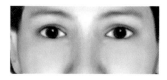 

Sharp, alert eyes   *Dull, lifeless looking eyes*

The Mountain Root, which is located between your eyes, all the way down the central axis of the face to the tip of your nose, governs the ages of 41-50.

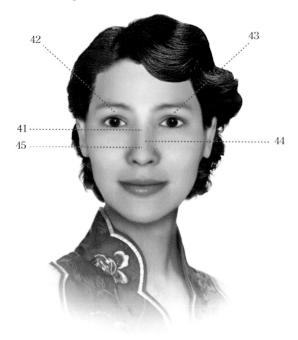

Senior Age (Ages 51-70)

Between the ages of 51-60, a person's luck is governed by the philtrum and their lips. The chin and the jaws influence a person's luck between 61-70.

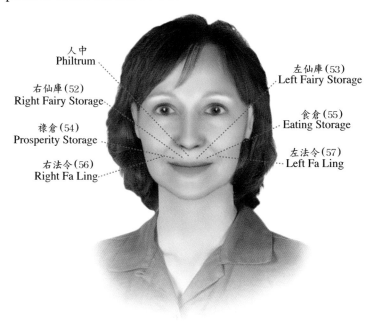

人中
Philtrum

右仙庫(52)
Right Fairy Storage

祿倉(54)
Prosperity Storage

右法令(56)
Right Fa Ling

左仙庫(53)
Left Fairy Storage

食倉(55)
Eating Storage

左法令(57)
Left Fa Ling

The mouth and chin are integral to determining what kind of old age a person will have. Now, in Chinese culture, we like to have a good old age or a good finish always. What is a good old age? It means to have lots of people around you to help you in your old age, filial children and lots of grandchildren. A bad old age entails living alone, with no children and no one around you, and being financially miserable.

Generally, we like broad, fleshy and round chins for prosperity in old age. A sharp pointy chin is often indicative of a lonely old age.

Broad, fleshy and round chin

Sharp pointy chin

Old Age (Ages 70 – 100)

Admittedly, most people who manage to reach 70 consider themselves extremely fortunate already and certainly, we practitioners do not have too many opportunities to perform destiny readings for senior citizens! But for completeness, I have included these age positions.

Okay, see, that wasn't so hard right? Now that you are familiar with the 100 positions, it is time to put some meat on the bones. In the next chapter, we will delve into the details of each of the 100 positions and what you can derive about your own fortune from your own face.

Chapter Three:
The 100 Positions

Face Reading, like Feng Shui and BaZi, requires a reference point. That is the purpose of the 100 year map of the face. In this chapter, I will introduce each of the 100 positions on the 100 Year Map of the face. The 100 Year Map is known as 'Bai Sui Tu' 百歲圖 in Mian Xiang.

The 100 year map of the face assigns every year of a person's life to a different part of the face. Different points on your face govern a specific age position or different phases of your life, while different features of the face govern different personality and character traits. Face reading practitioners often talk of 'eye luck' or 'ear luck' or 'nose luck' – this sounds strange if you do not understand the language of face reading. But if you understand face reading, you will know that a person in their thirties is going through eye luck. A person in their 50s is going through mouth luck. Each position of the 100 Year Map governs a different age in your life.

By using the 100 year map of the face, we can pinpoint a person's luck precisely by examining how well-developed (or under-developed) the area is. However, each position does not only represent a person's age luck, but also can be used to determine other personal attributes as well.

The first thing to remember is that the age luck positions for males and females is not always universal. Some positions are universal for men and women whilst some of the positions are not universal. Be conscious of this at all times initially until you are very familiar with the positions. Then you will be able to switch them appropriately for male and female readings.

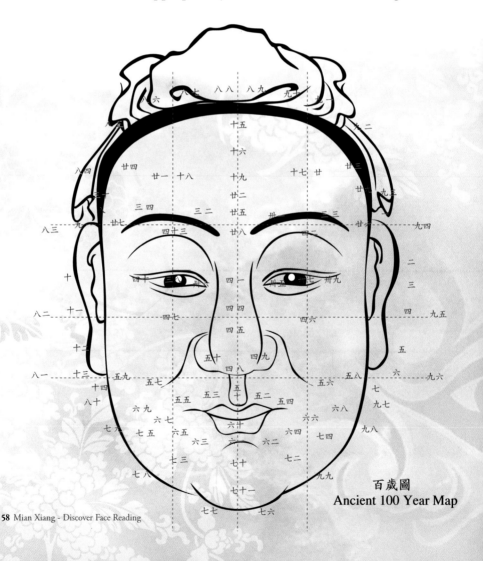

百歲圖
Ancient 100 Year Map

Remember this:

Females	Males
↓	↓
Always starts from the **RIGHT** side	Always starts from the **LEFT** side

Center line

Right   Left

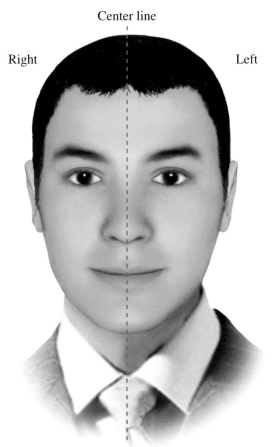

男左女右

Male left, Female right

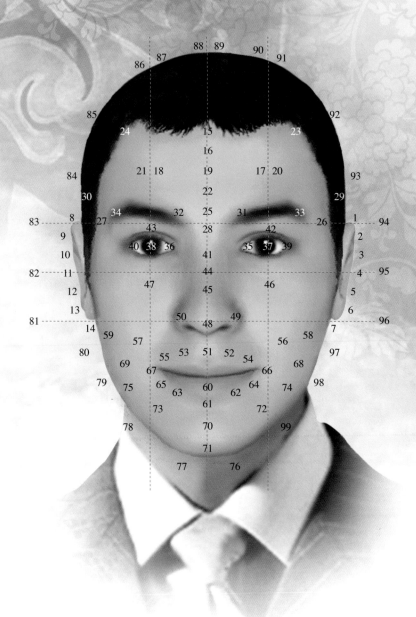

100 Year Map for Males

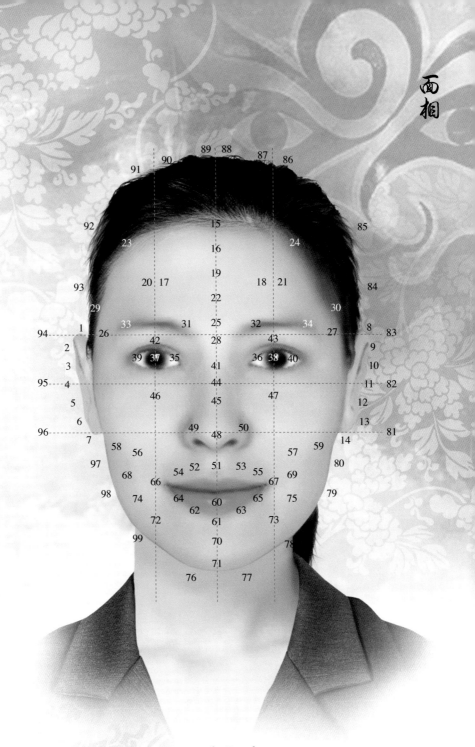

100 Year Map for Females

To help you with the learning, it is good to have a mirror on hand and also, as you go through the various positions, look in the mirror and point at the particular position on your own face. If you practice this as you go through this chapter, you will find by the end of this chapter you are very familiar with the 100 positions.

Each position on the face has a unique name but to facilitate learning, I have found, in the course of my Mian Xiang classes and public seminars, that it is easier to use numbers. I have indicated the Chinese names of these positions, and also provided an English translation of the names where appropriate. However, don't be too focused on the names or concerned if you can't remember them at this stage. Most of the names are verbatim translations from the original Chinese terms. Don't be too alarmed with some funny sounding names. I prefer to use verbatim translations and keep them as close to the original as possible.

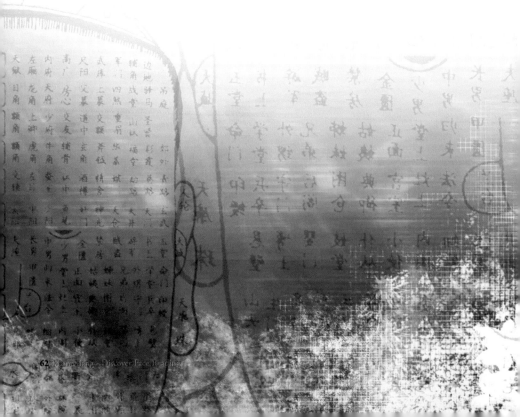

Ages 1-7 – Ear Luck

For ages 1-7, you must be sure to look at the correct ear. What am I talking about? In Mian Xiang, the 100 year map varies slightly, depending on the gender. For women, the 100 year map starts on the right ear, whilst for men, it starts on the left ear.

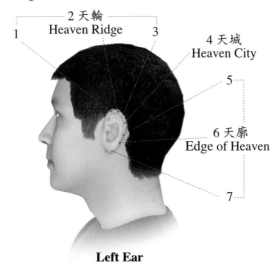

Left Ear

Positions 1 to 3 are known as the Tian Lun 天輪 (Heaven Ridge), position 4 is known as Tian Cheng 天城 (Heaven City) and positions 5, 6 and 7 are Tian Kuo 天廓 (Edge of Heaven). It's a lot easier to remember 1-7 just by the numbers – if you can remember the names, that's a bonus.

These 7 positions on the ear represent a person's earliest childhood days. A lot of character formation takes place during these years of a person's life. So if the ears are well-developed, chances are, the person received good care during his or her childhood and indicates the person will have a gentle, kind and loving personality. Conversely, an under-developed ear often belongs a poor or bad childhood, leading to the inability to give and receive love during adult life.

Chip on ear

When we look at ears, we are looking to observe several features - the completeness and definition of the ear ridge, whether the ears are set high or low, whether the ears are small or big and whether the ears are flexible or hard. The quality of the ears is essential to a person's luck in his or her early years.

If a child's ears are small and the ridges are not clearly defined, meaning there is a chip or indentation in the ear, this child will probably encounter misfortune between the ages of 1-7. If there is a chip in the ear, look at what age position it corresponds to and you can pin-point what year that misfortune will occur.

Now, logically, at the ages of 1-7, a child normally lives with his or her parents. Thus a misfortune at this age probably relates to the parents' well-being or financial stability.

So we can generally say that the misfortune probably involves poor living conditions, a harsh and hard childhood or poor parents who are unable to provide for the child.

A very quick way to look at a parent's luck is to look at their young child's ears. Now, you must be wondering – how do the two relate? If your child has poor quality ears, that means that you, his or her parent, has had to endure some hardship or tough times during this child's early years. If the child has good quality ears, then it means you their parent are not too badly off either!

Ears should not just have well-defined ridges, but should be high set. What do we mean by high set ears? High set ears are ears where the tip of the ear is higher than the eyebrow. Low set ears mean the tip of the ear is parallel or lower than the level of the eye. The best way to tell whether a person has high or low set ears is to look at his or her face, square on or from the side.

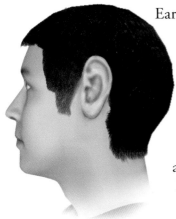

High setting ears

If the ears are higher than the eyebrows, this is a precocious child who can gain fame in life. High set ears also belong to people who are intelligent. Children with high set ears will also enjoy good robust health throughout their lives and they will be obedient, easy to manage children.

Good ears are those that cannot be seen when you look at a person from the front. We like ears to stick to the side of the head as far as possible – Dumbo-like protruding ears are not good ears. What do I mean by Dumbo-like ears? That means ears that appear clearly visible when you look at the person face on (like the picture on the right). Ears that stick to the side of the head belong to people who are more obedient and easy to bring up compared to those with protruding ears.

Ears sticking out visibly from front view

Ears for Ladies

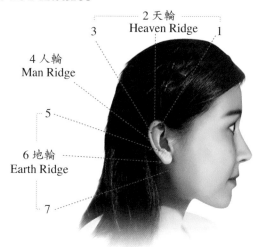

2 天輪
Heaven Ridge

4 人輪
Man Ridge

5

6 地輪
Earth Ridge

7

3

1

Right Ear

The right ear represents the ages of 1-7 for the females. Now, not only is the location of the age positions sometimes different for men and women, but often, our criteria for evaluating each of these positions differs depending on the gender.

The most important ear feature for women is the flexibility of the ear. If a woman has a stiff and inflexible ear, it denotes a hard life, most likely during the ages of 1-7.

The next most important feature of the ear when it comes to ladies is the Wind Gap. The Wind Gap dictates a person's attitude – a large or broad Wind Gap indicates a very open mindset, while a narrow Wind Gap indicates a conservative nature. When it comes to ladies, this gap should not be too broad.

Wind Gap

Generally, a conservative outlook is preferred for young ladies in Chinese culture. Parents with daughters who have wide Wind Gaps should be cautious with the liberties they allow their daughters. (Read: no late nights!).

Ages 8-14

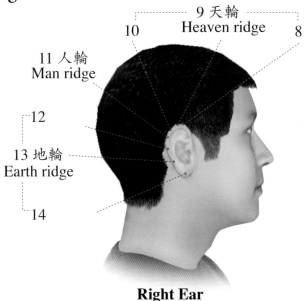

Right Ear

For males, the age of 8-14 is dictated by the right ear, while it is the left ear for females. The ages of 8-14 represent progression to youth – it is a transitional age, a person's teenage years. These are the formative years of a person that shape his or her character and nature – it is at these ages that children are easily influenced, are exploring their identities and are forming their ideas. So any problems that occur during these ages that are reflected in the ears may affect the person later in life or even throughout life.

The principles of evaluating the right ear (or left ear for females) are similar – we are interested in the ridges, the size of the ear and the length or height of the ear. If for example, the right ear is very thin, this denotes that during this age, that person was in poor health, in particular, mental health. This is because the ears represent Resource or thinking and thin ears suggest emotional disturbance.

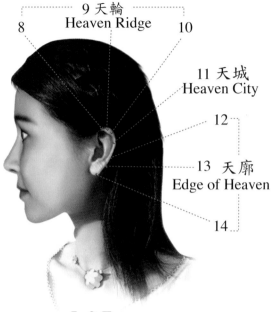

9 天輪
Heaven Ridge

8

10

11 天城
Heaven City

12

13 天廓
Edge of Heaven

14

Left Ear

If the tip of the ear is sharp or pointy, this suggests the possibility of emotional trauma caused by the parents, such as a divorce or a separation by parents. Now this is significant because it may lead to him treating his wife/spouse in the same way. A chipped right ear in Mian Xiang indicates psychological or emotional damage or issues that may trouble a person through adulthood. This is a combination of the fact that 8-14 is an impressionable age and the age where a person forms their character.

It is also important to compare the right ear to the left ear and to see if the setting of the ears is at the same level. If the ears are set at different levels or have different shaped ridges, this suggests a high likelihood of the person's parents being separated or divorced at this age AND there is a step-parent in the family portrait somewhere.

Sharp or pointy ear ridge

For girls, the colour of the ears is significant. The colour of the ears should be a shade lighter than the colour of the face (without make-up of course). If the ears are darker in colour, especially the left ear, this suggests that around the ages of 8-14, they are often ill or they are easily depressed, which is something that may affect them later in life.

Age 15 – The Fire Star

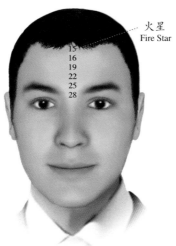

火星
Fire Star

15
16
19
22
25
28

The Fire Star is located at the center of the hairline, at the tip of the forehead. It is the highest point on the forehead and it should have no scar, no indentation or protrusion and be fleshy. Only if it satisfies this criteria is the Fire Star considered flawless. We like a high set Fire Star – how do you know if it is high or low set? Use the hairline as an indicator. If the hairline is closer to the eyebrows, then the person has a low hairline and a Fire Star that is hidden inside the hairline.

A high set Fire Star indicates a person who has good academic prospects and who will excel in his or her studies and enjoy good health. A low set Fire Star means that the age of 15 is 'inside your hairline' – this indicates a person who leaves school early to join the workforce or who is forced to leave school in order to support his or her family through work.

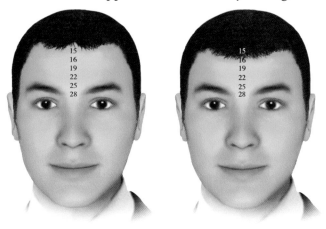

High Hairline   *Low Hairline*

For women with a moderately high and fleshy 15 position, they will have good luck at the age of 15 in terms of their relationships and education. They will get along well with their parents, teachers and peers and have good education luck.

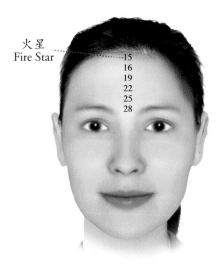

Age 16 – The Point of Nobility

To find position 16, you have to first, locate position 15. Now, one finger's width below position 15, is the location of position 16, as is shown by the diagram below. This position is the same for males and females.

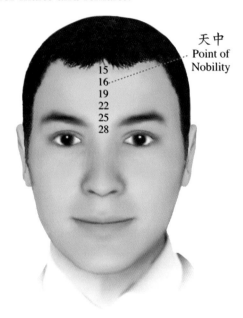

This position is very important in terms of a person's nobility, his or her stature and presence. People with nobility automatically command respect or have an aura of elegance. He or she will have a certain exquisiteness (nothing to do with his or her looks) that give him or her a commanding air, a certain regality and charisma.

We don't like a low, punctured, indented or scarred 16. These are people who not only find they cannot command respect or lack charisma, but are people who often inspire instant dislike!

I'm sure you can think of a few people you know who are like that – check their position 16 and you'll find a definite problem there.

Scars, punctures, indentations or a low set 16 also indicate people who have poor family luck. They often have a lot of problems and obstacles when it comes to education and may not even have the opportunity to pursue their education to a tertiary level.

Now, take a look at the picture below. This is called the Golden Chicken Pecking the Bright Hall Formation, where the hairline touches or 'pecks' the position 16. In Western culture, this is known as a Widow's Peak. This denotes a lady who will come out to work early in life, or perhaps furthers her education abroad alone or a lady with a difficult and complex relationship with her father.

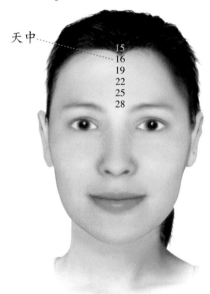

金雞照明堂

"Golden Chicken Pecking the Bright Hall" Formation

Nobility is important for women because this ensures they will be gentle elegant wives. Women with dented position 16 tend to have very robust characters, and are usually very outspoken. They will usually have problems with their fathers and potentially, the men in their lives. At the age of 16, these ladies will have difficulty concentrating on their studies as they are often easily distracted.

I want to just briefly give you a little taster on Qi colour. Qi colour is not the person's skin colour, but the impression at first glance, of the person's skin and skin colour, without make-up. We are interested in the colour that permeates the area. If a woman has dull Qi colour at position 16, this denotes a lack of elegance, a certain brashness or boldness and a lack of genteel ways.

Age 17-18 – The Sun and the Moon

Position 17 is called the Sun Point and position 18 is called the Moon Point, as indicated in the diagram below.

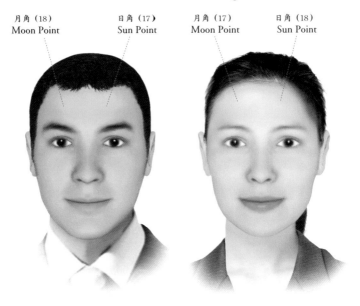

月角（18）
Moon Point

日角（17）
Sun Point

月角（17）
Moon Point

日角（18）
Sun Point

The Sun represents the father and the Moon represents the mother – hence, these two positions govern the quality of your relationship and affinity with your parents. The Sun and Moon positions also relate to help from your parents and whether or not they give you assistance in life.

Scars, lines and dents on these positions indicate a poorly-developed Sun and Moon. Hence, such people are usually people who make it on their own or who are self-made. A well-developed Sun and Moon by contrast indicates a person who receives financial assistance from his or her parents or who inherits a business from them.

For ladies, if at the Sun position, the skin colour is gloomy and at position 16, there is a Golden Chicken Pecking the Bright Hall, this denotes very poor affinity with the father or a lady who brings bad luck to her father.

Let me briefly explain this concept of 'bad luck'. In Chinese culture, when parent and child do not see eye to eye, or the child is rebellious, this is regarded as 'bad luck' to the parent. This comes from the notion that peace brings money so arguments at home mean that there is no wealth coming into the house. It does not literally mean bad luck!

Age 19 – The Heavens

Find position 16 on your face and now, find the position that is one finger's space below that position. This is the position known as The Heavens and represents the age luck for the age of 19. It is between the Sun and the Moon, smack in the center of the forehead.

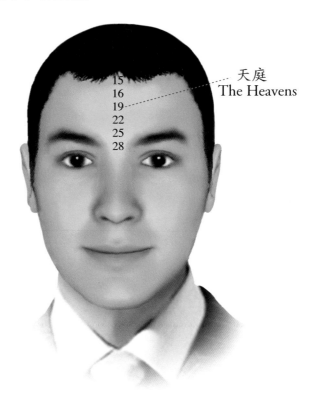

While the 100 positions each represent a person's luck at a certain age, the positions also have a dual significance, which is to indicate certain personality traits or characteristics. Whilst position 16 relates to a person's elegance and aura of elegance, position 19 relates to the ability to behave elegantly, to carry themselves well, to radiate class, even if they are penniless. Position 19 gives a person dignity, stature and an air of genteelness, whether they were born into a rich family or a poor one. For example the Queen of England, Elizabeth II, has an air of dignity and stature, no matter what the newspapers write about the Royal Family.

Good politicians need to have an excellent position 19 to ensure that they can win support, without ever saying a word. Fame and respectability also depend on a good 19. Good position 19 here means that this spot is fleshy, unscarred and the skin colour is balanced.

Position 16 and 19 in many respects go hand in hand. You need both to have the potent combination of presence, authority, class, dignity and elegance, all the requirements of a well-respected pillar of society and person who commands respect and admiration. Finally, the quality of position 19 depends heavily on the quality of positions 17 and 18 for the Heavens must be supported by the Sun and Moon.

This type of reading is known as Hun Liu Fa (混流法) or Multiple Position Reading. In Multiple Position

Reading we read several positions together to determine the outcome. As this is a beginner's book, I will focus on Ding Liu Fa (定流法) or Fixed Position Readings where we only focus on one position to derive a meaning. However, where appropriate, I will show you some Hun Liu Fa (混流法) techniques as well, so you can gain an understanding of how detailed a study of Mian Xiang can be.

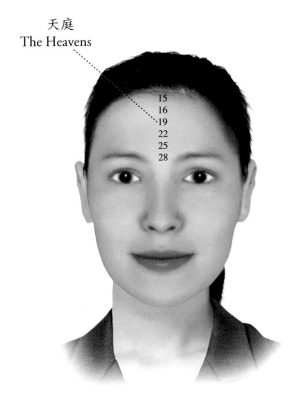

天庭
The Heavens

15
16
19
22
25
28

Position 19 is particularly important for ladies because it relates to their ability to gain the respect of their husbands but also, it relates to 'recognition' by the husband. Now, you might be wondering, why is Joey talking about recognition – of course a husband recognises his wife surely? In Asian societies, it is not uncommon for men to have more than one wife or an unofficial second wife. When a woman has no 'recognition' from her husband, it means she is regarded as a second wife. We say she has no recognition because her husband will not 'recognise' her in public as his wife.

A mole in position 19, for example, generally indicates that the woman will lack the respect of her husband or she will have marriage problems.

Now, here's a sampling of how Hun Liu Fa (混流法) or Multiple Position Reading works. Mistresses or second wives usually have a poor position 19 and a small nose. If the position 19 is very bad, it is very unlikely the man will be willing to divorce his wife and marry the mistress. Hence, she will not get 'recognition' from the husband.

For ladies who come for consultations with a weak 19 position, a Destiny Consultant will usually advise her to marry a divorced man. See, modern society lets us get around some of these problems. By marrying a divorced man, in law, you are the second wife, but you are still recognised in public as 'the wife'. This is the way to overcome the weakness of the poor 19.

Ages 20-21 – Left and Right Assistants

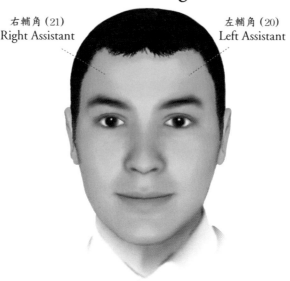

右輔角 (21)
Right Assistant

左輔角 (20)
Left Assistant

These two positions are called the Left Assistant and Right Assistant and are located next to the Sun and the Moon positions, as per the diagram above.

Right and Left Assistants represent benefactors and determine whether or not a person can find or seek help from family members. Now, the Left and Right Assistants must be read in tandem with the Sun and the Moon. If the center of the forehead bulges, the Sun and Moon and the Assistants will droop or sink in naturally – this indicates a person who cannot get help from family members and is unable to get help from them even when he seeks help.

If position 20 and 21 is dented, this indicates poor luck when you leave the house, especially when travelling. For example, you lose documents and even the police are unhelpful or unsympathetic. You always meet difficulties and do not seem to be able to find people who can help you out.

For the ladies, the age positions of the Left and Right Assistants are reversed but also, these positions are read mainly in regard to marriage. This is because traditionally, 20 and 21 was the age of marriage for most young ladies.

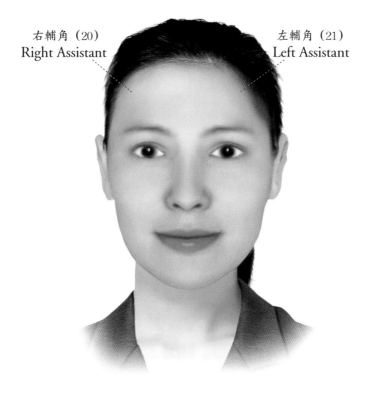

右輔角（20）
Right Assistant

左輔角（21）
Left Assistant

Positions 20 and 21 must be examined in tandem with the bridge of the nose and the shape of the mouth when it comes to women. Now, what a woman wants is a husband who is reliable and who she can count on and depend on to take good care of her. If position 20 and 21 are unfavourable, this means bad benefactor luck. If a woman also has a low or knotted nose bridge, or a downward sloping mouth, this denotes a lack of assistance from spouse, a lack of passion in the relationship and a poor quality husband.

Age 22 – The Confidence Point

Position 22 is also known as Si Kong 司空. It is located 1 finger's space from position 19, the Heavens. This is a universal position for both men and women.

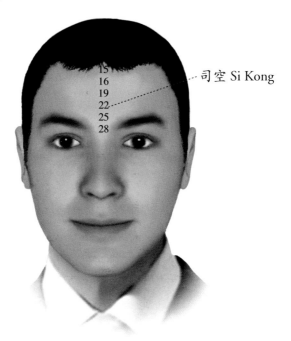

司空 Si Kong

Position 22 is an important position to evaluate on every person's face because this position ties in directly with a person's self-confidence, self-esteem and sense of respect for himself or herself. Whether or not a person has belief in his or her own abilities and self, whether a person has a positive or negative perception of himself or herself, all depends on position 22.

Timid people, people who always feel inadequate, people who always feel they have the short end of the stick or always feel they are at the receiving end of unfavourable deals (even when it is extremely favourable to them) are people who usually have sunken, scarred or bulging position 22. The deeper the dent or the more prominent the scar, the more defeatist the attitude and the lower the person's self-esteem.

Do you know of someone who is immensely wealthy or doing very well by most people's standards, but yet, deep inside, or even outwardly, he feels and constantly remarks about how he lacks achievements? People with a problem with position 22 often feel inadequate and will always compare themselves unfavourably to other people, often on very minor issues.

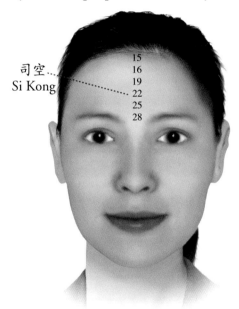

Women with a scarred or dented position 22 are usually fixated with what their boyfriends or spouse think of them. These are the women who are always seeking the approval of their spouse or boyfriends. A sunken or scarred position 22 can also lead to a woman becoming anorexic or being obsessed with how she looks.

If position 22 bulges instead of being sunken, this is the mark of a vain woman, who will also enjoy showing off. So if you wish to avoid a high maintenance wife, avoid marrying a woman with a bulging 22! This is also applicable to men – if a man has a bulging position 22, he is likely to be vain and flashy with his appearance. A man with a bulging 22 will want a trophy wife on his arm and a Rolex watch on his wrist for the whole world to see.

I am sure at this point, you are wondering – how do I tell if a position on the face is bulging? Well, think of it this way: if you can tell it is dented, you can tell it is bulging! In Mian Xiang, obvious features – like scars and sunken positions – are easy to discern but that does not mean the subtle signs are not there. They just require a little more 'training'. Focus on looking at the details, and looking at people from different angles. The key is to avoid negative thinking – keep trying and soon, you will realise you see things that you never saw before in people!

This position relates directly to a person's ability to gain fame and reputation, and bring pride to the family name and their ancestors, what the Chinese call 'Ming Qi' (名氣). Bringing repute to your family name is considered a great achievement in Chinese culture. If position 22 aligns directly with the tip of your nose, this means that you will make your family name famous and make your ancestors proud of your achievements.

Now, a direct alignment between position 22 and the tip of the nose is not easy to achieve and not easy to discern either. You need to visualise an imaginary line from the tip of the nose aligning in a straight 180 degree alignment to position 22.

Often you will find that this line is not exactly 180 degrees. Those who do have a 180-degree direct line between the tip of their nose and position 22 are regarded as having a special feature on their face.

People with low position 22 (meaning, low hairline) cannot hold high government or public office. This of course all makes sense. How many politicians do you know have low self-esteem or lack confidence?

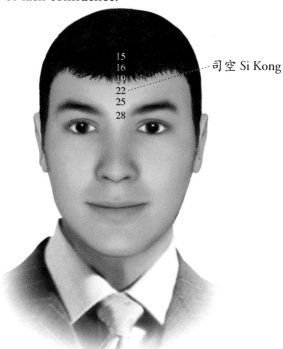

Low hairline, low position 22

However, don't be too disheartened if your 22 is low. Always remember the classical saying in Mian Xiang: "面由心生 Xiang You Xin Sheng" – the face features comes from the heart. If you can change your outlook and attitude, you will find that slowly your face will also change.

Ages 23-24 – The Sky Horse

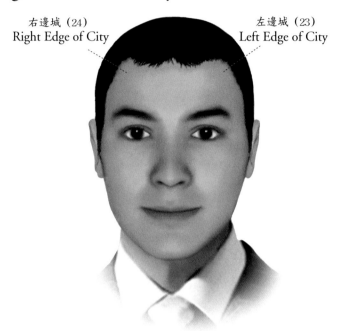

右邊城 (24)
Right Edge of City

左邊城 (23)
Left Edge of City

The positions for the ages of 23 and 24 are located at the two corners of the foreheads and are known as the 'Edge of The City.' These two positions are also known as the Sky Horses (驛馬). This age position is not universal for males and females – for males, position 23 is on the left, while position 24 is on the right, and vise versa for females.

Why do some people have no difficulty migrating to another country whilst other people never seem to be able to fit in? How come some people take to working in new countries with ease while other people suffer culture shock and just can't stand being away from home? It all comes down to the position 23 and 24. A high and broad position 23 and 24 indicates a person who can or will work in faraway places or who can successfully migrate to another country and work. People with low or covered positions 23 and 24 are people who cannot migrate successfully as their Sky Horse or Travelling Palace is not of good quality.

People with fleshy, moist and fresh looking skin at position 23 and 24 are people who can travel and make money from business activities that require them to travel. These are also people who will benefit from joint-ventures that involve overseas components or partners.

Face Reading can also be used for daily evaluation of a person's luck or fortune. How do you know if a person will have an accident during a trip or encounter problems during a journey? Let's say, it's not convenient at that time to plot a BaZi chart and what you need is a quick answer.

The answer is to check the Sky Horse. A pimple or a blackish Qi appearing on the Sky Horse is the strongest indication that travelling will bring misfortunes such as car accident. If at that point in time, the eyes are dull and there is black Qi on the nose and/or pimples on the nose, we can conclude that the person will probably experience a car accident that does not cause death but will probably involve substantial financial loss.

Right Edge of City
右邊城
(24)

Left Edge of City
左邊城
(23)

For women, positions 23 and 24 are reversed. Now, when Face Reading practitioners check position 23 and 24, it is usually when we are asked in a consultation (or more often, during casual conversations after my talks or seminars), as to whether or not a lady's spouse will be a foreigner or how they will meet their Significant Other.

Dark Qi at the Sky Horse

右邊城（23）
Right Edge of City

左邊城（24）
Left Edge of City

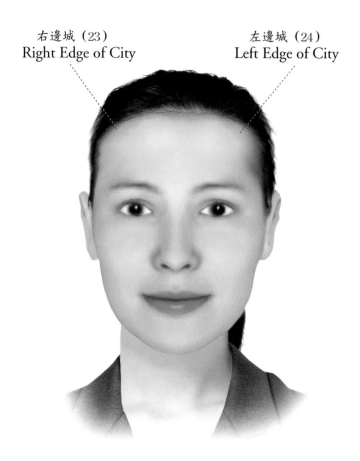

If a lady has a high position 23 and 24, she will very likely meet her Significant Other while travelling for education or working in a foreign posting. On the other hand, if a lady has a low setting 23 or 24 or the hairline grows downwards and obscures the position 23 and 24, this indicates that the lady will not have to step a foot out the door to find her Significant Other. Instead, her Significant Other will come looking for her.

Age 25 – Direct Center

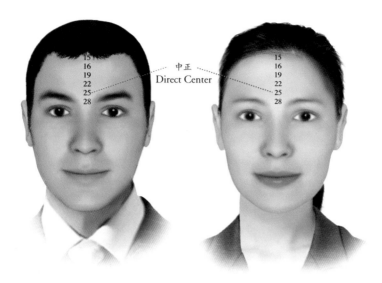

The position for a person's age luck at 25 is located one finger's space below position 22. This position is universal for both males and females. This position is also known as Direct Center (中正). We like this position to be flat, the skin to be moist, no protruding bones and no scars or lines crossing it. Now, when I say flat, I mean flat. Not sunken, not protruding and not bulging.

Direct Center relates to a person's grounding and his or her level-headedness. It also relates to a person's ability to appreciate what he or she has in life. A sunken or protruding Direct Center position belongs to a person with extreme viewpoints. These are people who can be obsessive in their likes and severe in their dislikes – there is no sense of balance in their lives.

Now, while generally a flat 25 indicates good luck at 25 for a person, we have to use Hun Liu Fa (混流法) or Multiple Position Reading to evaluate the 'extent' of how good position 25 will be for the person. Position 25 must be read in tandem with the ears, the Mountain Root and the eyebrows. All these features must support position 25 for the age luck at 25 to be considered 'good'. If the ears, the eyebrows and the Mountain Root are supportive of 25, we can say that a person will gain a promotion or pay rise at the age of 25.

Let me share with you one more Hun Liu Fa technique when reading position 25 – if the position 25 is dented, combined with spear eyebrows and the person is a female, then you can expect this person to experience a major set back at the age of 25, most likely a set back related to the person's relationship.

Ages 26-27 – The Tomb and Grave

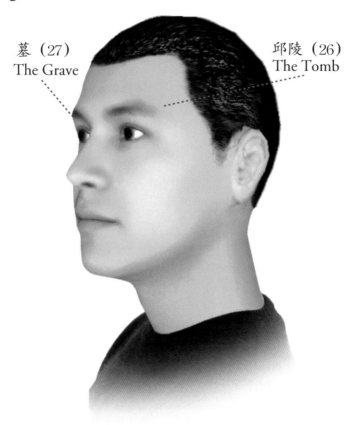

墓（27）
The Grave

邱陵（26）
The Tomb

Whenever you think of positions 26 and 27, I want you to think of headaches. This way, you will be certain of never forgetting where these two positions are located. When you have a headache, you press your temples to relieve the pain. Positions 26 and 27, known as Qiu Ling 邱陵 (Ancestral Tomb) and Zong Mu 宗墓 (Ancestral Grave) are located at your temples, diagonally above the tip of the eyebrow. The age position is reversed for ladies.

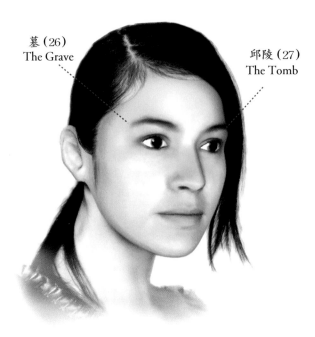

墓 (26)
The Grave

邱陵 (27)
The Tomb

These positions tell us about the person's inner intentions and their sense of altruism and comradeship. Is this person selfish and motivated only by their own self interest? Or are they the one for all, all for one 3 Musketeers type? Do they think of others as well as themselves? From position 26 and 27, we can tell. We are looking for fleshy and clear skin at positions 26 and 27 with no fine lines nor fine veins crossing this area.

So you might be wondering: why does the name of the position refer to ancestors? For two reasons: Firstly, if your ancestors were good people and you had a good upbringing, you will appreciate the importance and significance of being honourable and upstanding because this has been inculcated in you early on in life. On the other hand, if someone has not had a good upbringing or their background is poor, then to them, honour and integrity, indeed, comradeship, are probably not of significance.

Positions 26 and 27 are called Ancestor Grave and Ancestor Tomb also because these positions really do have a connection to your ancestral tomb and grave. If you have a hairline that is tight and close to the forehead, covering the temples, this suggests your ancestral grave is in an unfavourable Feng Shui position, traditionally. If these positions are sunken, it is likely the grand ancestral tomb is also sunken or flooded by underground water.

According to Mian Xiang texts, if this position is fleshy and the skin colour is bright and fresh, this means your ancestors are akin to guardian angels, extending their hand from the Heavens to guide you on the right path.

Age 28 – The Resource Hall

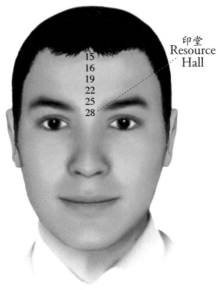

Position 28 is the most important position in the face, for both males and females. It is known as the Life Palace or Yin Tang 印堂 (Resource Hall). The Resource Hall is located between the eyebrows and is universal for both males and females.

Face reading begins with reading the Life Palace. If the Life Palace is broad and spacious and fleshy, not bony, the person's quality of life is good. What do I mean when I say quality of life? Different people have different ideas of what quality of life means – for some, it means good health, for others, good relationships and for most of us, enough money for all our wants and needs, and more. But have you considered that quality of life might be poor if a person has enough money for ten lifetimes but lingering ill health or loneliness in life? The Life Palace is covered in more detail in Chapter Four – for this section, I will focus on reading position 28 in relation to the person's age luck.

28 is an important age in Chinese Face Reading because it is the transition point towards the middle stage of a person's life. This is a catalyst point in everyone's life – if at 28, a person is doing well, this suggests smooth sailing and good luck ahead. If things are challenging and difficult at 28, then generally, that person can expect to have to keep going uphill through the middle stage of his or her life and more tough times and days ahead.

A good Resource Hall is broad – we like it to be two fingers wide. A narrow Resource Hall, where the eyebrows are tightly squeezed together, means the Resource Hall is restricted and this indicates a person who is narrow minded. A broad Resource Hall belongs to an open-minded person who is generous and sincere.

For a snapshot evaluation of your luck on any particular day, just look at the Life Palace. If the Life Palace is patchy and dark, that means that your luck on that day is poor and misfortune is likely to be hot on your heels all day!

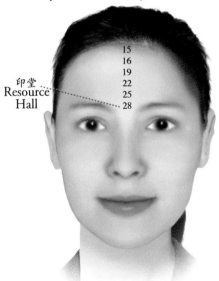

Location of Life Palace

Age 29-30 – The Forest of the Face

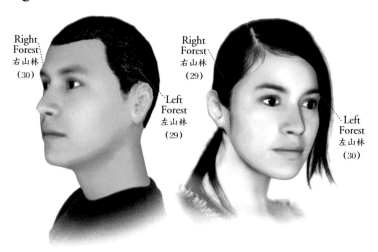

Right Forest 右山林 (30)

Left Forest 左山林 (29)

Right Forest 右山林 (29)

Left Forest 左山林 (30)

Positions 29 and 30 are located inside the hairline, about 1 inch above the ear ridge, as indicated by the pictures above. These two points represent the ages of 29 and 30 and are closely associated with 26 and 27. These positions do not influence the characteristics of a person generally and relate more to the Feng Shui of a person's ancestral tombs.

These two positions must be read in relation to position 28 so we have to use some Hun Liu Fa (混流法) or Multiple Position Reading technique when looking at positions 29 and 30. If position 28 has a needle piercing it (a thin line that looks like a needle piercing the position), this is considered a position 28 that carries Sha Qi. If there is a chipped or broken eyebrow and the eyebrows are very dense, this indicates a person who will face a life threatening major accident at 30.

If the Mountain Root is low, and there is a tight 28, and position 29 and 30 is sunken, this suggests at 28 or 29, there are health problems or accidents that cause poor health.

Ages 31-34 – Brow Luck

The ages of 31-34 are represented by the eyebrow as a whole. Ages 31 to 32 are represented by the head of the eyebrow while ages 33 and 34 by the tail of the eyebrow. Which is the head and which is the tail? Look at the pictures above. Remember, these positions are not universal for men and women. For men, 31 is represented by the left eyebrow head, 32 by the right eyebrow head, 33 by the left eyebrow tail, 34 by the right eyebrow tail. For ladies, the sequence begins with the right eyebrow head.

Positions 31 and 32 are very important in reading and evaluating a person's fortune through their face. The eyebrows represent a person's basic character and nature. Are they crude and aggressive? Or gentle and kind? Are they nice to furry creatures? Will they be a business partner who stabs you in the back? It's all in the eyebrows.

Individuals who have a commanding imposing presence usually have winged eyebrows (the eyebrows resemble a set of wings) or eyebrows that grow upwards. By contrast, timid and cowardly sorts have eyebrows that slope downwards.

Individuals with spear head eyebrows are often stubborn and opinionated and their lack of flexibility or overly strong opinions will cause them problems between 31-34.

Spear-headed eyebrow

Eyebrows that are broken by lines (such as a cut or a scar) indicate problems at 31 and suggest their affinity with siblings is not so good. Eyebrows that are thin and sparse denote people who are weak-willed, lack perseverance and have little personal drive – they will not be able to achieve their goals or will simply lack ambition. They may even be aimless during their thirties.

Chip in the eyebrow

Now, as you have noticed already, the criteria for women and men, in Mian Xiang, is quite different. What is good for a man is not necessarily what we want to see on a woman. Certain positions have universal 'good' and 'bad' features but most of the positions have distinct and different criteria for each gender.

For ladies, thick eyebrows are most undesirable. Ladies with thick eyebrows, especially if the head of the eyebrow is dense, lack feminine characteristic. This is not to say they will be butch but rather, we can say they lack a measure of gentleness and polish or finish that one would expect from a woman. They also lack the meticulousness that women commonly exhibit. In Cantonese, we say such women are Chou Lou (粗魯) – crude is not quite correct, lacking feminine wiles is perhaps the best way to describe it. As

Lady with very thick eyebrows

such, these women usually have difficulty getting married or have challenges in their personal relationships at that age.

In Mian Xiang, a man's face should have male or Yang features, a woman's face should have Yin or feminine features. So when you have features regarded in Mian Xiang as appropriate for females, on a man's face, what do you get?

A metrosexual man!

If you see a man with overly sparse eyebrows, these are men who are often overly-concerned with minor details and will nitpick at the smallest things. Ladies, these are men who will probably argue with you over the colour of the curtains in the house, or fuss over spots on the wall! A good eyebrow, when it comes to men's eyebrows, is one that is neither too sparse nor too dense but

Man with thin and sparse eyebrows

most importantly grows in a uniform direction – this indicates favourable progress career-wise at the age of 31-32 and for single men, a likelihood of getting married at these ages.

Positions 33 and 34 are represented by the tails of the eyebrows. Again, remember that these positions are reversed for women.

Earlier, I mentioned that we like eyebrows to be not too sparse, but not too dense either. Now what you might be wondering is - what is too dense? Too dense means the roots of the eyebrow hair are not visible. Sometimes, a person can have dense eyebrow hair but the roots are still visible. In such instances, the person is usually someone who has helpful friends or siblings who are useful in times of difficulty.

Overly dense eyebrow

We don't like the eyebrows to be too long either. If they are thick and long, and touch the temples, these are individuals who are often too generous to their friends. These are people who will buy round after round of drinks at the pub for their friends, never mind that it means they go home broke for the month! They will also lend their last dollar to their friends, if their friends ask for it.

Now, you may be curious to know, how is this principle derived? Remember, positions 26 and 27 represent a person's sense of comradeship, altruism and how he treats his friends. A thick set of eyebrows generally denotes an overly strong sense of comradeship, a need to show-off and constantly demonstrate support to friends.

Sparse eyebrows at positions 33 and 34 belong to people who cannot save money because they spend it too quickly. How do we tell if eyebrows are sparse? Usually this is indicated by an eyebrow where each strand grows very far apart from another.

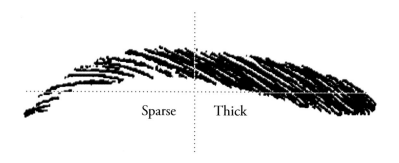

Sparse   Thick

Eyebrows can also be sparse and thin. This is not a good combination. It indicates a man who has no guts and lacks the ability to capitalise on opportunities, even when presented to him on a silver platter. While this will improve once the person passes the age of 34, it will remain a problem for life unless he makes a conscious, psychological effort to be more assertive and go-getting.

Ladies, pay attention to a man's eyebrows if you want to know about his character before you start dating him or walk up the aisle with him. If the eyebrows are dense at 33 and 34, you can expect to be number two in his life - his friends and siblings are the people who he will lavish his money on. If his eyebrows are sparse at 33 or 34, he cannot save money so perhaps you should take charge of the finances. A good husband is one with consistent eyebrow density throughout the entire length of the eyebrow, indicating a person who is focused and organised, has guts and drive in life.

Ages 35-36 – Great Yang and Great Yin

Whereas the eyebrows represent a person's character, the eyes tell us about his or her heart. When someone does not look you straight in the eye when he or she speaks to you, or his or her eyes flick left or right when he or she speaks to you, this is a big hint that his or her intentions are not pure or true. Their dealings, their conversation and their actions, lack sincerity. Eyes represent the heart. Where the eyes are not straight, the heart is not pure.

Position 35 is known as Great Yang (太陽) and 36 is Great Yin (太陰). 35 is on the left eye tip, 36 on the right eye tip, when it comes to men. The positions are reversed for ladies.

太陰 (36)
Great Yin

太陽 (35)
Great Yang

太陰 (35)
Great Yin

太陽 (36)
Great Yang

When looking at position 35 and 36, it's like looking at a diamond: we're looking for clarity and colour. The tips of the eyes should not be red nor should we see little red veins at this point. If you see little red veins on your child's eyes, you can be sure they won't be coming home with an A if there's an exam coming up soon. Red lines on the positions 35 and 36 often indicate failure in examinations.

Of course, most people don't face exams at the age of 35 and 36. So what do red veins at these positions mean for a grown up? Well, if you think about it, life is one long examination. Every day we are tested – by people around us, by our clients, by our customers, by superiors, by spouses or girlfriends/boyfriends.

The concept of 'failing exams' at 35 means these people are always failing whenever they are in a situation that calls for an evaluation. People with red veins on the tips of their eyes are the people who never seem to get good remarks during their performance appraisals (lose out on the promotion), never seem to do well at job interviews (can't get a new job that pays better) or worse, fail at their relationships or can't seem to get married! These are the people who get told 'no' when they propose to their Beloved.

Ages 37-38 – Middle Yang and Yin

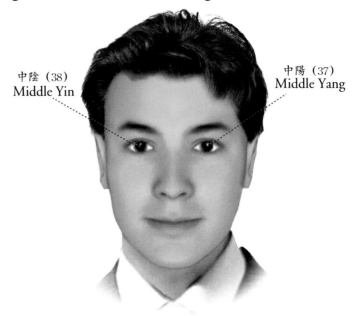

中陰（38）
Middle Yin

中陽（37）
Middle Yang

Positions 37 and 38 are represented by the moving palaces of the eyeballs. Now, we like positions 37 and 38 to be sharp, alert and moving – they must be spirited. This tells us the person is lively, sharp and 'with it' so to speak.

Now, you may have met some people who have eyeballs that do not move. The eyes are dull, sleepy, lifeless and they always seem to be staring out into emptiness. These are people who exemplify the phrase, the lights are on but no one's home. These people will also experience bad luck at 37 and 38.

If the eyeballs are watery and moist, this indicates a person who is very sentimental or emotional. It also suggests that at the age of 37 or 38, their personal relationships are undergoing some changes or they are faced with some issues that call for change. If the pupil of the eye is very large, to the point that the eye has more black than white, this indicates a gullible person who is often plagued by emotional issues or challenges. For instance, being troubled by relationship issues.

For ladies, the eyeball whites and pupils must be clearly defined. What does clearly defined mean? This means that the whites of the eyes are not jaundiced or have a yellow tinge. Jaundiced eye whites or yellow tinged eye whites indicate poor 'eye luck'. The ages of 35-40 will bring many difficulties and great changes. They may change jobs, or change spouse if the eyes lack clarity.

If the eyes are jaundiced or yellow tinged but there is clarity, then this indicates changes that are for the better. Clarity here refers to colour definition between the iris and the eye-whites. Some eye-whites are yellowish or dull in colour - this means there's no clarity.

中陰 (37)
Middle Yin

中陽 (38)
Middle Yang

Ladies with watery and sad looking eyes are ladies who are in a marriage that is unhappy. They may have a smile on their face, but their eyes will tell you a very different story so always look closely at the eyes and don't be deceived by the smile.

Now, when we look at the eyes, especially for ladies, we usually must look at the space under the eyes, which is known as the Children's Palace. I will cover the Children's Palace in more depth in the next chapter on the 12 Palaces. However, I want to talk a little bit about the Children's Palace here because it relates to the subject of eye luck and women.

All women have experienced bags under their eyes or dark circles under their eyes, but if a woman has this despite 12 hours of sleep every night, this is a cause for concern. In Mian Xiang, this indicates poor affinity with children.

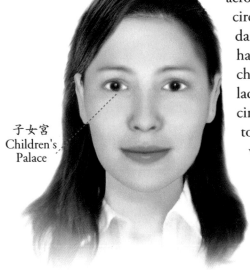

子女宮
Children's
Palace

People with children who are ill or children who are disabled also tend to have lines across the eyebag and permanent dark circles. If parents have a lot of lines and dark circles, this can also indicate they have difficult children or problematic children. Often, I see this in a lot of ladies. If the children are fine, dark circles or bags under the eyes belong to paranoid parents, parents who are very protective of their children.

Did you know that face reading can also tell us a lot about a person's health? For example, blue ring around the eyeballs indicates a person with heart-related ailments.

Ages 39-40 – Lesser Yang and Yin

少陰（40）
Lesser Yin

少陽（39）
Lesser Yang

少陰（39）
Lesser Yin

少陽（40）
Lesser Yang

Ages 39 and 40 are represented by the ends of the eyes and are known as Lesser Yang and Lesser Yin. The ends of the eyes should slant upwards slightly for good luck. Downward slanting ends denote bad luck at the ages of 39 and 40. We also do not like to see red veins crossing the tips of the eyes or sagging upper eyelids.

If the upper eyelid sags and covers the 39 and 40 position, these are individuals who are possessive or who are never satisfied with any outcomes, no matter how good, and this is the source of their problems at 39 and 40.

Age 41 – The Mountain Root

山根 (41)
Mountain Root

The Mountain Root is a very important position – it is the next most important position after the Life Palace. The Mountain Root dictates a person's principles and virtues. It is a person's storage of confidence, personal drive and perseverance. This position is located in the same place for males and females.

If the Mountain Root is too high, the person is over-confident and egotistical. If it is too low, that person has a problem with reality. It is best to be broad, stable and straight. If the Mountain Root is low, that means a difficult and hard life, with no help from others. These people have to count on themselves throughout their lives and will be self-made people.

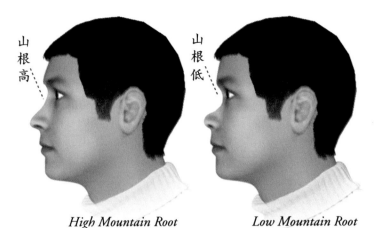

山根
高

山根
低

High Mountain Root   *Low Mountain Root*

If the Mountain Root is high (but not too high), this denotes a person who easily overcomes negativity and can turn adversarial or unfavourable situations into opportunities. These people will never experience a dead end in their lives because they have an optimistic outlook and also, luck just seems to favour them, even in their lowest moments. Usually, high and strong Mountain Roots belong to people who are healthy or keep themselves healthy.

山根 (41)
Mountain Root

Ladies with a low Mountain Root have weak self-esteem and may have lots of constant health problems. Ladies should also be careful of a line crossing the Mountain Root – this represents an adulterous relationships if the line is thin. If the line is thick, this means a health issue or lingering health problem. For men with a low Mountain Root, they are well advised to marry later in life because the first marriage is unlikely to be good and may end in divorce.

Ages 42-43 – Windows to the Soul

Positions 42 and 43 are found at the eyes and is a universal position for both males and females. Now with eyes, we look for a slightly different criteria compared to the face. Eyes, unlike say the nose or the cheeks, can move. Have you heard of the phrase dancing eyes? Or people who have animated eyes? A lot of facial expression is often conveyed through the eyes.

光殿（43）
Guang Dian

精舍（42）
Jing She

That is why, when we look at the eyes in the context of Mian Xiang, we are interested in the spirit of the eyes – the liveliness, the alertness that can be seen in the eyes. A person's eyes should look sharp and bright to be considered good.

We don't like the eyes to be sunken generally and puffy swollen looking eyes are not good either. Sunken eyes suggest emotional problems, difficulty with expressing oneself or discontent with romantic relationships. Eyes should not look puffy, like a half open clam. This does not mean the eyes are half slit, rather, imagine a clam that has its shell half open – it is a kind of sleepy, lidded look. Puffy, half open clam-like eyes belong to people who are always getting themselves into trouble. You know, people who are always at the wrong place at the wrong time and doing the wrong thing.

Sleepy and puffy eyes

If a lady has dull, watery eyes and the area around the eyes looks dark and puffy, it is almost certain that the lady is in a bad emotional relationship due to poor communication with her spouse, has an unloving spouse or has a spouse that does not understand her.

光殿（42）
Guang Dian

精舍（43）
Jing She

Age 44-45 – The Health Positions

Positions 44 and 45 are located on the nose – position 44 is located on the nose bridge and is called Nian Shang 年上. Position 45 is called Shou Shang 壽上 and is also found on the nose. These are universal positions for both males and females.

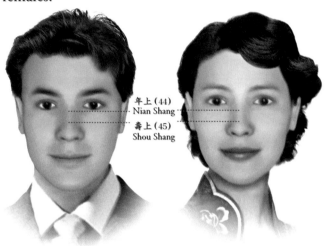

年上 (44)
Nian Shang

壽上 (45)
Shou Shang

Both these positions relate to health but the more important question you should be asking is: whose health does the position relate to? Position 44 relates to the health of the person whose face you are reading. It should be meaty, not bony, straight and unbroken, which indicates good robust health.

As you have noticed by now, not every age luck position is governed by that particular position alone. Sometimes, a position is qualified or evaluated with regard to other positions. So when looking at position 44, it is also essential to look at the nose tip. We like a broad and rounded nose tip to accompany a meaty and unbroken position 44 for position 44 to be considered good.

Face reading requires us to be able to observe those persons not just from the front, but from the side, when they are relaxed, and when they are smiling. A line or lines across position 44 when a lady smiles indicates the likelihood of problems giving birth. A dark patch on each side of position 44 also suggests problems with the back.

Position 45 also tells us about the health of family members or people in the same home as the person whose face we are reading. Position 45 will show dark Qi or dark patches if there are people in the person's home who are ill or sick. A line going across position 45 is not a good sign for health – this indicates lingering illness or persistent health problems.

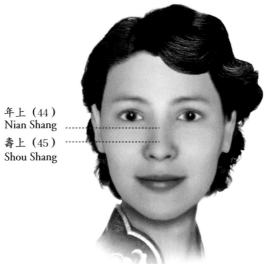

年上（44）
Nian Shang

壽上（45）
Shou Shang

Remember how the positions represent not just age luck but personal characteristics or relate to an aspect of the person's life? When we look at position 44 and 45 for ladies, we are also checking their relationship luck. The nose bridge must be neither curved in nor bulge out for ladies to have a good husband and enjoy a good relationship with their spouse!

Age 46 – 47 – The Power Bones

右顴（47）
Right Cheekbone

左顴（46）
Left Cheekbone

Positions 46 and 47 are located at the cheekbones. The cheekbones are known as the Power Bones (權骨) in Chinese and thus, cheekbones represent not just a person's age luck at 46-47, but his or her will-power and ability to wield power.

破
顴
紋
Scar
or
Line

For good luck at 46 and 47, the cheeks should be fleshy. We don't want any lines growing from the tip of the eyes and cutting across the cheekbones. This is called Breaking the Power Bones and denotes great problems at the age of 46 or 47, which may lead to a significant loss of wealth or bankruptcy. We also do not like any moles on the cheek either – now, since I have included a special chapter on Moles in this book, I won't cover the relevance of moles on the cheek. If you're curious, then peek to Chapter Five!

Breaking The Power Bones

Fleshy cheekbones, along with a well-developed nose, are the kind of facial features you see on people who wield tremendous power and influence in an organisation. These are features you see on CEOs of big corporations, high level politicians, such as Presidents and Prime Ministers, and of course, military generals.

How do you know if a person is a nice gentle warm person or a ruthless hard-nosed person? Look at their cheeks. People with bony cheeks are ruthless and forceful people, who are not afraid to use their fists to solve a problem. People with fleshy cheeks on the other hand, are usually more gentle, sentimental and value friendship. If the cheekbones are not fleshy and are set high in the face, these are people who have strong fighting spirit – don't try to threaten these people into submission. These are people who, as we say in Chinese, are not afraid to die!

Strong and big cheekbones

Generally, we do not like ladies to have high cheek bones, in particular, cheekbones that are higher than the nose. High cheekbones that sit higher than the nose tip and which protrude indicate a woman who controls or over-powers her husband. If the cheekbones are simply higher than the nose but do not protrude, then the woman is a mistress or second-wife.

Sagging cheekbones are also not good – these features belong to people who are uncharitable and generally mean and nasty.

Age 48 – The Point of Conscience

The position for age luck at 48 is the nose tip. This position, besides governing a person's luck at the age of 48, also tells us about this person's conscience and inner nature. Whether or not a person is cunning and the type to seek to gain at other people's expense, or whether he or she is the good-hearted, honourable sort, can be determined from a person's nose tip.

準頭
Nose tip
(48)

In western imagery, witches and wizards are often depicted with sharp pointy noses. This is not too far from the way Chinese Face Reading views people with sharp pointy noses. In Mian Xiang, a pointy sharp nose denotes a person with a wicked heart who is ruthless and ungrateful. These are not people you want to have as your friends (although they might probably make good henchmen for your organisation). People with fleshy, bulbous nose tips on the other hand, have no 'poison in the heart' 鼻頭有肉心無毒 as we say in Chinese. They will be virtuous and grateful in their deeds.

You will discover in Chapter Four, where I talk about the 12 Palaces on the face, that this position forms part of the Wealth Palace. The nose tip should be rounded not just to ensure a person has a good conscience, but also because this denotes good wealth prospects and potential. The fleshier the nose tip, the better the person's potential to accumulate wealth. Naturally, a thin or bony nose tip means a reduced wealth capacity.

Before anyone rushes out to the nearest plastic surgeon to have their nose enlarged, you should know that an overly large nose does not mean you will be rich beyond your wildest dreams. You cannot (as is popularly done these days at plastic surgeons) walk in with a picture of Donald Trump's nose and say, I want my nose to look like that, and expect to own the Taj Mahal or Trump Tower tomorrow.

It doesn't work like that I'm afraid.

Here's the catch, the nose must fit the face. You can't stick a big nose on a person with a small face or squeeze a big nose in between narrow cheekbones. Your nose size must be proportionate to your face. If a nose is too big and the face is small, this is known as a Lonely Mountain and signifies loneliness in marriage – either you are a widow or widower early in life or your spouse is never at home.

準頭
Nose Tip
(48)

I want to briefly touch on Qi colour with regard to the nose, just to pique your interest a little. How do you know if a business deal you are negotiating or closing today will be profitable? Ah, look at the Qi colour on your nose. There is an ancient Mian Xiang saying: One drop of yellow is one drop of wealth – every time there is yellow Qi on your nose, wealth luck has arrived!

Ages 49-50 – Wings of Wealth

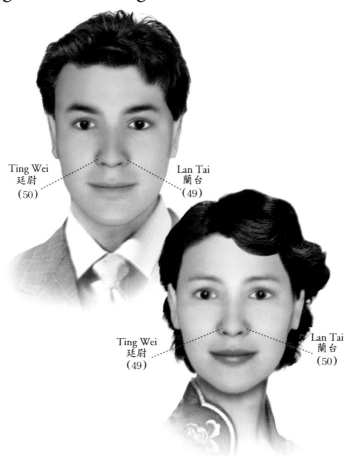

Ting Wei
廷尉
(50)

Lan Tai
蘭台
(49)

Ting Wei
廷尉
(49)

Lan Tai
蘭台
(50)

Ages 49 and 50 are represented by the nose wings. The positions are reversed for males and females, as indicated in the pictures above. Nose wings should be demarcated otherwise this indicates difficulties at 49 and 50. The person is filled with confusion at the crossroads of his or her life. If the nose wings are clearly defined, the ages of 49 and 50 will be an easy time.

The nose wings also represent a person's ability to make money – it is not the Wealth Palace per se but it is one of the features that must be considered when evaluating the Wealth Palace, as explained in Chapter Four.

For good money making ability, a person should have extended, broad and thick nose wings. These are individuals who have multiple streams of income and are usually tycoons who run conglomerates with multiple interests or wide ranging businesses. Those who have non-defined nose wings are individuals who only make income from one kind of job or industry. The nose wings tell us whether a person can handle multiple jobs or earn money from many avenues or whether that person should stick to just one thing.

For ladies, the above applies but it is also important to check to see if their nostrils are upturned. Upturned nostrils indicate the person is a gossip and a backbiter, someone with a very sharp tongue. Such a person may find that they are ostracised socially due to their remarks or experience a hard downfall as a result of things they have said about other people.

Upturned nostrils or exposed nostrils are also the mark of people who are hopeless at saving money. This is because when the nostril is exposed, the Wealth Palace is regarded as 'leaking' wealth. How do you know if a person's nostrils are upturned? It is best to look at that person's face from the front – if you can clearly see the two 'black holes', then the nostrils are definitely exposed.

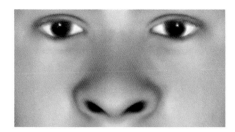

Exposed nostrils

Age 51 – The Middle Path

The position for the age of 51 is the philtrum, which is the portion directly under the center of the nose that runs all the way down to the tip of the center of the lips. It is known as Ren Zhong 人中 – the term I use is Middle Path.

人中
Philtrum

This is an extremely important position when evaluating a person's face. The philtrum is the position that governs the transition from middle age to old age. It is the period of crossover, from the upper part of a person's life to the lower

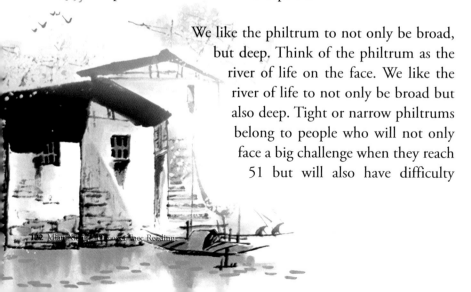

part of his or her life. This is one of those 'make-it-or-break-it' facial features. The philtrum determines whether you lose everything you have worked hard to acquire and achieve at 51 or whether you can 'take it all with you' into your old age. This is a universal position for both males and females.

In Chinese Astrology and Face Reading consultations, clients will sometimes ask if they have a 'big challenge' (Jie 劫) at any point in their life. Now, Westerners may not be familiar with this concept so I will elaborate a little. A 'big challenge' in life is like a mid-life crisis, a personal Waterloo. The iceberg in the path of your Titanic. Position 51 tells us whether or not a person will face a major challenge at 51, whether or not he or she can handle that major challenge and also, whether or not he or she will have a short or long lifespan. Position 51 also relates to a person's wealth and whether or not that person will be able to take his or her wealth into old age.

You will notice that in almost every discussion on the different age positions, generally, the preference is for 'fleshy' rather than sunken or bony or thin. Generally, we do not like any part of the face to be sunken in or indented.

The philtrum is the ONLY exception.

We like the philtrum to not only be broad, but deep. Think of the philtrum as the river of life on the face. We like the river of life to not only be broad but also deep. Tight or narrow philtrums belong to people who will not only face a big challenge when they reach 51 but will also have difficulty carrying their wealth forward into their old age. A scar or line on this position when the person smiles indicates a major obstacle that is potentially life threatening when the person reaches the age of 51.

Often in BaZi consultations, women (and increasingly, men) want to know: can I have kids? The philtrum is an excellent non-invasive way to tell if a person will have trouble having children.

For women, the philtrum is a good way to check fertility as it relates directly to the reproductive organs. A mole on this position, a scar on this section or a person with a harelip or repaired harelip will have difficulties giving birth or have health issues related to their reproductive organs. A tight philtrum, where the philtrum is narrow and needle-like, indicates difficulty giving birth or difficulty having children. A short philtrum with a mouth that curves upwards indicates problems with the reproductive organs. For men, a tight or narrow philtrum indicates some problem with their plumbing or a problem with their sperm count or sperm.

There's a saying in Chinese face reading – if the Ren Zhong is flat, your children are mediocre. Unfortunately, it is not easy (and may have counter-productive results) to adjust or improve the philtrum through cosmetic surgery so usually, for ladies or gentlemen with a philtrum problem, I will advise the use of Feng Shui to help them start a family.

Ages 52-53 – Fairy Storage

右仙庫
(53)
Right Fairy
Storage

左仙庫
(52)
Left Fairy
Storage

右仙庫
(52)
Right Fairy
Storage

左仙庫
(53)
Left Fairy
Storage

Ages 52 and 53 are represented by position points located on the left and right of the philtrum. This is not a universal position – so age 52 is the left of the philtrum for men, and age 53 is the right. This position is reversed for women. Now, the terms 'Fairy Storage' (Xian Ku 仙庫) and 'Food Storage' (Shi Cang 食倉) are a bit deceptive when used to describe positions 52 and 53. Don't take the words literally – we are not talking literally about a place where you store food. Rather, positions 52 and 53 refer to a person's prosperity.

In Chinese culture, food represents prosperity. Whenever a Chinese person meets another person, he or she will always ask: have you eaten? Now, despite the obvious implications of the statement, we are not interested in what they had for lunch. Rather, because eating is considered prosperity, hence this is a coded way of asking 'how have you been doing lately'.

In Chinese philosophy, prosperity is not just about money. Prosperity refers to someone who, despite being average or moderately wealthy, has the opportunity to eat many different kinds of food and experience many epicurean delights.

In modern times, starvation is relatively rare in most developed societies so the question becomes: what is the quality of life and quality of food that you eat? Are you living an epicurean existence? Or are you a philistine who can't tell one cut or meat from another?

People who lack prosperity are not necessarily those who are poor or starving, but rather, these people do not know how to enjoy their wealth with epicurean delights. These people are those with bony or thin position 52 and 53.

For ladies, you do want a man with a thick and fleshy 52 and 53. Why? This denotes that your husband takes care of you and you will have a good life. In Chinese, we call this "Yi Shi Wu You 衣食無憂" literally easy life, no starvation or hardship.

On the ladies face, we don't want any white patches on this part of the face, or lip hair growing at this section either. This indicates not only will you never be able to appreciate the finer things in life, but you will not even be able to appreciate having money! And, such a lady will most likely have to take care of herself all her life.

面相

At my public talks and seminars, I frequently get asked about moles around the mouth and lip area. Moles are covered in detail in Chapter Five but let me give you a teaser here. (If you are impatient, then skip straight to Chapter Five!)

Mole above the lips

There are moles and there are marks In Mian Xiang, we distinguish between moles and marks. Moles are considered moles, if the area protrudes slightly, is black and has a different texture. Marks on the other hand, are brown and have no discernable texture. A mole at position 52 is known as an Eating God mole. These people, rich or poor, have endless opportunities to enjoy the best food in life and the most epicurean and exotic food experiences.

Ages 54 and 55 – Eating Storage

Positions governing the ages of 54 and 55 are right next to 52 and 53, just above the tip of the lips as in the picture below. These two positions are known as the Eating Storage and are closely related to positions 52 and 53.

Eating Storage

In addition to governing a person's age luck at 54 and 55 it also relates to the ability of a person to enjoy his or her wealth. Position 52 and 53 relate to a person's opportunities to enjoy epicurean experiences and good food, positions 54 and 55 relate to whether a person knows how to seek out epicurean delights but more importantly, whether or not that person can create opportunities for himself to gain wealth.

When evaluating the Eating Storage, it is also important to look at the borders of the mouth. A mouth with clear borders and one that is always 'smiling' is a truly good mouth in Mian Xiang. If positions 54 and 55 are well-developed, the person's mouth will always seem to be smiling, even when he or she is relaxed or not deliberately smiling.

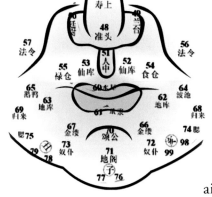

There should be no lines from the lips growing upwards because this indicates bad financial luck at the ages of 54 and 55 and possible bankruptcy at that age. If both 52 and 53, as well as 54 and 55 are thin, it means a lingering incurable illness at that age. We also don't want to see dark patches of Qi at the mouth, as this suggests illnesses related to the kidneys, problems with blood circulation or water-related ailments.

Ages 56-57 – The Laughter Lines

Positions 56 and 57 are represented by what we call the Fa Ling 法令 or Laughter Lines. They are called Laughter Lines because they are usually prominent or very visible when a person smiles or laughs.

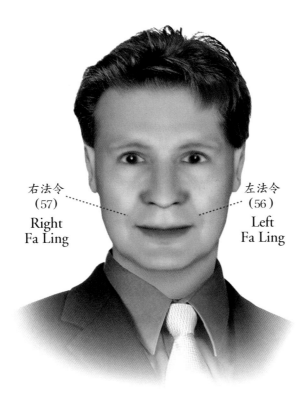

右法令
（57）
Right
Fa Ling

左法令
（56）
Left
Fa Ling

There are two things to remember about the Fa Ling: first, it should not be seen before a person reaches the age of 45, and secondly, you WANT Fa Ling lines to appear. If the Fa Ling appears before the age of 45, this indicates a life of suffering or extremely hard work. But, it is important to have good long and moderately deep Fa Ling – long Laughter Lines are a sign of a long life.

Besides indicating a good long life, the Fa Ling relates to a person's reputation and name. Normally, persons with high status in society have deep and broad (meaning, they are not tight to the mouth) Fa Ling which are clear, distinct and unbroken. If the Fa Ling is broken or faint, then at 56 or 57 there will be bad luck. If the Fa Ling is clear and unbroken, then at 56 and 57, there will be good fortune, smooth luck and increased status.

Gambling luck is something I always get asked about whenever I do BaZi consults (and usually, this question is frequent during the peak of gambling season, at Chinese New Year). Now, this is not something easy to answer especially without the benefit of a BaZi chart but if you are asked by someone on whether or not he or she will be lucky that day, look at the Fa Ling. If the Fa Ling is greenish or blackish in appearance, any wager is unlikely to produce a good outcome.

For ladies, the Fa Ling is very important as it relates to their ability to enjoy a good, easy and luxurious life, without the need to have to work hard. Now, remember, in the Chinese context, for a lady to have to work hard is not a good life. A deep Fa Ling indicates that a lady's life is stressful and laden with pressure.

右法令
(56)

Right
Fa Ling

左法令
(57)

Left
Fa Ling

We also do not like to see a break in the Fa Ling – this indicates the likelihood of broken limbs. For males, it signifies breaking your leg at that age. Depending on which Fa Ling line it is (right or left), a Face Reading practitioner can also tell whether it is the left or right leg that will be broken. We also do not like to see the Fa Ling curving into the edges of the mouth – this is called Snake Entering the Mouth 藤蛇入口 and indicates death caused by lung or stomach cancer.

Ages 58 and 59 – Tiger Ears

Ages 58 and 59 are located at the jaw joint, along the mandible. This position is known as Hu Er 虎耳 (Tiger Ears). Now, it is called the Tiger Ears but it doesn't have anything to do with tigers. Like many of the Chinese names used in Chinese Metaphysics, the names are sometimes more 'romantic' to make them memorable.

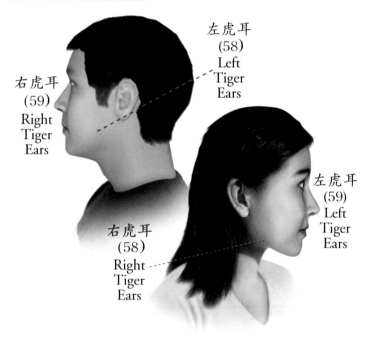

左虎耳
(58)
Left
Tiger
Ears

右虎耳
(59)
Right
Tiger
Ears

左虎耳
(59)
Left
Tiger
Ears

右虎耳
(58)
Right
Tiger
Ears

Besides governing the age luck of a person at 58 and 59, positions 58 and 59 govern a person's gratitude. How do you know if a person you help will remember what you did for him or her or repay you for your kindness? Look at the Tiger Ear position or positions 58-59.

If the jaw joint area is bony, then the person has no sense of gratitude. If it is bony or the jaw bone protrudes there, this person is ungrateful and not sentimental. Now, we must not confuse a lack of gratitude with the person being 'bad' or evil. Some people are sincerely ungrateful – this means that they are not aware that they are being ungrateful or they simply assume that whatever has been done for them need not be repaid back.

In Chinese, we have a saying that directly translates to "bring your eyes to see people and you'll find you see so much more of a person, even after having known them for a long time". Looking at a person's jaw line will tell you whether or not a person is going to be grateful for what you do. However, one should never be calculative in life unless it is a major business association. After all, we do not just help people in the hope of getting something back in return. One good turn, as they say, deserves another but that's not why we do something for someone in the first place.

The quality of positions 58 and 59 also depends on the quality of the ears and also a position slightly above the jawbone, called the Center of the Life Gate. If a person has what we call pearl lobes (the lobes resemble small pearls sticking out), then the person's attitude will improve with age and they will gradually learn how to be more grateful to people, reducing the impact of the protruding jaw joint.

People without pearl earlobes and a protruding jawbone at positions 58 and 59 are usually ruthless and merciless. If this portion is bony or sunken, the ears have no lobes, and the Center of the Life Gate is sunken, this denotes major health issues at the age of 58 and 59. If the person has all the above features and the nose is sharp and pointy, this suggests that the challenge faced by the person at 58 or 59 will be financial.

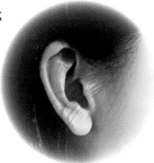

Good ear lobes

Age 60 – The Water Star

Age 60 is represented by the tip of the lips and is universal for both males and females. It is also known as the Water Star or the pearl of the face.

水星
Water Star

In the study of the Five Elements, water relates to emotions and a person's feelings. Accordingly, the mouth tells us about a person's innermost feelings. In short, whether or not a person is happy or sad can be seen from the lips, in tandem with the eyes.

When we look at position 60, we are evaluating the mouth as well. We like a mouth that is a little bit big. In the old days, small mouths belonged to people who had no money, and thus no food. Today, people with small mouths are usually people who have a hard life and much illness in old age.

You might be wondering – how do I know if a mouth is small or big? You need to not just look at the mouth in the context of the face (it should be proportionate) but also, look at it with regard to the nose. A small mouth is a mouth that is smaller than the nose width.

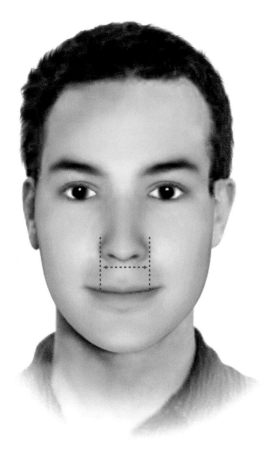

Big mouth: When mouth is evidently larger than the nose

The lips should meet at a point, in order for a person's luck at 60 to be good. If there is no point, that person's luck at 60 will not be good.

水星
Water Star

Lips should also have a clear border and the corners of the mouth should point upwards, even when the person is not smiling. If the mouth has no clear borders and slopes downwards at the corners, it denotes loneliness at 60 and also indicates an emotional person.

For ladies, the lips are mainly evaluated on the thickness of the lips. We don't like lips that are too thin on a lady – this is because thin lips belong to people who are ruthless, unsentimental and don't value the relationships they have with people. Women should have moderately plump lips, indicating a gentle and sentimental nature.

However, we don't want overly thick lips either as this indicates they are likely to be flirtatious. Ladies, beware of men with thick lips – they are generally lascivious in nature!

We can tell many other things from a person's lips but because this is a beginner's book, I'll stick to the bare basics. My next book will cover lips in greater detail.

Age 61 – Cheng Jiang Position

This position is known as Cheng Jiang (承漿) and is located at the center of the lower lip, as indicated in the picture below. This position is universal for both males and females.

承漿
Cheng Jiang
(61)

Again, we want a fleshy position 61, indicating a good retirement and a smooth transition into old age. Why is this so important? Well, we must understand a little bit about Chinese culture to appreciate the context of Face Reading sometimes. Old age, in Chinese culture and in Face Reading, is about having plenty of children and grandchildren by your side. This is considered true prosperity. A bad old age is one where you are alone and lonely.

If you have a 'hole' at position 61 (such as an indentation) or 61 is scarred, it represents poor social status and a short life, suggesting the person may not be able to live till the age of 70. A thin or scarred or indented 61, or a 'gloomy 61', meaning this area looks 'dark' and shadowy, indicates health problems at this age, loneliness or an old age spent drowning your sorrows in alcohol. A fleshy 61 means a household full of filial children and grandchildren who are always around you and much happiness.

承漿
Cheng Jiang
(61)

However, position 61 must always be considered with regard to the laughter lines or Fa Ling or Laughter Lines. If the Fa Ling is short, position 61 does not matter. If the laughter lines are long, then position 61 is evaluated.

Ages 62-63 – Earth Storage

Position 62 and 63 are just beside position 61, below the lower lip. (See picture below). It is known as Di Ku 地庫 (Earth Storage). These two positions not only represent a person's luck at the age of 62 and 63, but also whether or not a person will have assets or wealth to leave behind as inheritance for the next generation.

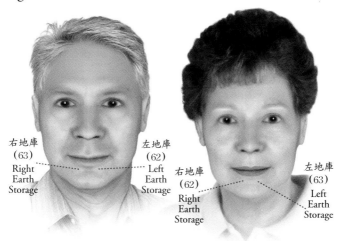

A bony 62 and 63 is highly unfavourable for women. A thin or bony 62 and 63 means being widowed without any money. This outcome is especially likely if the woman also has a bony nose. This is because a bony nose indicates a lonely old age – combined with a bony 62 and 63, indicates being lonely and without money.

If this position is sunken or scarred, the ears have no lobes, and the Resource Hall is narrow and the eyes are dark, this indicates death at 62. But if all these positions are good, then the person's life will be long, with many children supporting him or her in retirement age.

Ages 64-65 – Old Age Supporters

Positions 64 and 65 are located in close proximity to positions 62 and 63, as the picture below shows. These two positions relate to a person's old age and whether or not you have Noble People (Gui Ren 貴人) in your old age. We like a fleshy 64 and 65, which indicates that you have many members of your extended family and many friends by your side at this age.

鵝鴨
(65)
Er Ya

陂池
(64)
Pi Chi

We like flesh below the lips, not a thin bony section here. Also, it is important to see if the mouth is a sad mouth or a happy mouth. If the area below the lips is thin and the person has a sad mouth, this person will experience a substantial loss of wealth at the age of 64 and 65, which will definitely be a hard and harsh blow.

Position 64 and 65 are very close to the mouth, which is known as the Water Star of the face. Accordingly, we like the skin around this area to be plump and moist, not dry and crumpled. The area around the Water Star, like the area around a stream, should be moist and wet, not dry. A dry Water Star indicates health problems, mainly related to circulation, such as kidney problems or blood problems.

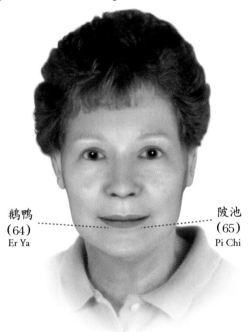

鵝鴨
(64)
Er Ya

陂池
(65)
Pi Chi

Positions 64 and 65 must always be considered with regard to the person's mouth shape and the Laughter Lines or Fa Ling and also the colour of the lips. If the position 64 and 65 are plump and fleshy and the lips are a healthy moist pink colour, then the person's old age is prosperous and good.

The 100 positions, while governing luck at that particular age, also relate to a person's overall luck in life. So for example, if there is no flesh or it is bony at 64 and 65, and the chin is flat, this is indicative of a person who has a short lifespan.

Ages 66-67 – Lip Edge

The ages of 66 and 67 are represented by the corners of the mouth. 66 is the left lip corner for men, the right lip corner for women, as indicated in the pictures below.

右金縷
(67)
Right
Gold
Point

左金縷
(66)
Left
Gold
Point

右金縷
(66)
Right
Gold
Point

左金縷
(67)
Left
Gold
Point

Now, the corners of the mouth should not be rounded like a clown's mouth. We do not like to see the smudged lipstick look at the corners of the mouth. Instead, we want the corners of the mouth to point upwards. Even when a person is not smiling, the corners of the mouth should point upwards, as if they are smiling. This indicates a happy, optimistic person with a positive outlook on life. People with corners of the mouth that point downwards are people with emotional problems or who are always sad.

This position should be a little bit white because this position is called Jin Lu 金縷 (Gold Point) – the colour of gold is not gold, as we all commonly think, but is white. So this portion of the face should be pale or slightly pink – it should not be dark.

Have you ever wondered why some people annoy you with their every statement, no matter how innocuous? And yet other people, saying exactly the same thing, do not grate on your nerves? The Jin Lu represents the ability to be persuasive and the power of speech. Whether or not the things you say annoy people, or make them stop and listen to what you say, depends entirely on the person's Jin Lu.

Ladies who are married should know that having a good Jin Lu is really worth its weight in gold! If you have a good Jin Lu, your husband will listen to your every word and let you have your way, without you having to raise your voice.

We do not like the Laughter Lines or Fa Ling to touch the corners of mouth. People who have laughter lines that touch or stick to the corners of the mouth are stubborn as mules and very difficult to persuade and it is hard to get them to change their minds. But if a person has a fleshy Jin Lu and a long Fa Ling that does not touch the corners of mouth, you are looking at a person who has status and influence and whose words and pronouncements carry weight and influence.

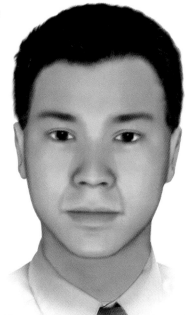

Fa Ling too close to Jin Lu (Gold Point)

Ages 68 and 69 – The Dimple Zone

The general principle in face reading is that we do not like the face to be sunken generally, the philtrum being the exception to this rule. Sunken portions are seen as 'missing sections' of the face.

Dimples may look cute on kids and may enhance a person's attractiveness (and did you know people with dimples are better drinkers?) but they also mean some difficulties at the ages of 68 and 69, especially if the dimples are very prominent and deep. Dark coloured skin at 68 and 69 also indicates a person is a worry wart and often worries for no good reason.

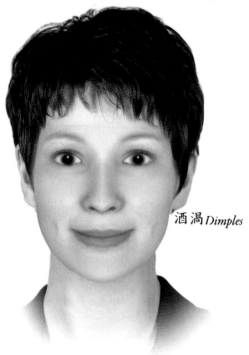

酒渦 *Dimples*

By contrast, if positions 68 and 69 are fleshy, that means good health, happiness and prosperity in the family and it is a portent of a long life.

Age 70 – The Chin

The center of the chin represents the age luck position for the age of 70. This is the same for both men and women. This position represents old age and what we want is for this position to be fleshy, smooth and not wrinkly. At the same time, we need to check that the person has lively and alert eyes, showing good eye spirit, and the voice is not frail or wispy. The voice does not have to be loud or even forceful, but should be clear and audible. A wrinkly chin, and a wispy weak voice, indicates health challenges at 70 for the person.

下巴
Chin
(70)

Now, you might be thinking – at 70, most people should have wrinkles. Not true! Take a look at Queen Elizabeth, look at Warren Buffet, look at Li Ka Shing – you will see that their faces are not lined and wrinkled, despite their old age. And it has nothing to do with facials and everything to do with good fortune in their old age and a nice chin!

Age 71 – The Earth Corner

地閣
Earth Corner
(71)

This position is also known as the grave of the face as it is located the lowest point of the face. We like breadth at this point, not a pointy 71. The Earth Corner should be a gentle rolling hill, not a rocky outcrop.

A good Earth Corner is broad and fleshy, indicating a person who has great wealth or great status, and enjoys respect and high position in society. The Earth Corner should protrude gently – we don't want it to stick out too much, but we also do not want it to recede inwards. A gently protruding 71 indicates a prosperous and luxurious old age, with lots of filial children or grandchildren who are always around you.

For women, we prefer this position to be rounded while for men, slightly squarish. If a woman has a square chin, it means she has to work even in her old age and that is not considered a good old age for a woman. If the chin of the woman is squarish and sharp, this indicates a stubborn person and one who has to work hard in her old age. Rounded chins that do not protrude sharply belong to tai-tais or ladies of leisure, which is the life a woman of 71 should be enjoying!

地閣
Earth Corner
(71)

Scars or lines at position 71 indicate health challenges at this age or problems with children. It may also indicate a troubling or lingering illness at that age. A cleft at the chin, which in face reading indicates tremendous creativity, also indicates problems at 71.

Ages 72-73 - The Hired Help

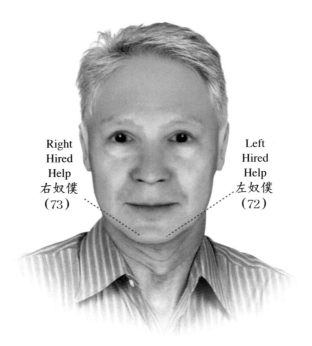

Right Hired Help
右奴僕
（73）

Left Hired Help
左奴僕
（72）

Ages 72 and 73 correspond to the Hired Help Palace, which is also covered in Chapter Four, on the 12 Palaces. The Hired Help Palace essentially relates to a person's ability to be an employer or a boss and whether or not that person will have good staff or children or students.

In a person's old age, it is considered a good life in Chinese culture if he or she has lots of people around who are able to help him or her get out and about. A good and prosperous old age is about having servants and filial children. Hence, the ages of 72 and 73 correspond to a person's Hired Help Palace.

This portion should be smooth, broad and unlined. It should also be fleshy, and the skin should not cling to the bones. Crumpled skin, thin skin or lines at this position indicate staff problems in your old age (a bad maid for example), disobedient or unfilial children or illness at the ages of 72 and 73.

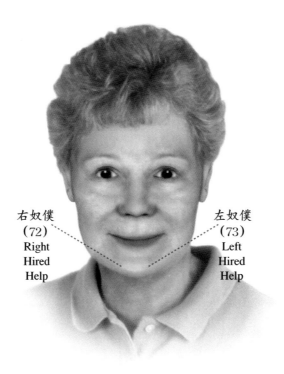

右奴僕
(72)
Right
Hired
Help

左奴僕
(73)
Left
Hired
Help

Qi colour in this area should not be black or green as this indicates possible accidental death or death by unnatural causes, especially if coupled with protruding eyes. If a man's eyes protrude, his Adam's apple is very prominent and there is green or black Qi at position 72 and 73, this indicates death by accident, such as a motor vehicle collision.

Ages 74-75 - The Jawbone

For the ages of 74 and 75, we look at the person's jawbone. This position should be fleshy, not bony and there should not be any protrusions. The jawbone or jaw hinge should not jut out or protrude. A good position 74 and 75, meaning one that is fleshy as opposed to bony and dull coloured, complemented by pink and healthy looking lips, indicates a pleasant, prosperous time at the age of 74 and 75, surrounded by pleasant friends and company.

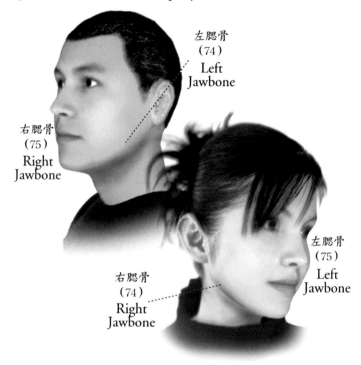

左腮骨
(74)
Left
Jawbone

右腮骨
(75)
Right
Jawbone

左腮骨
(75)
Left
Jawbone

右腮骨
(74)
Right
Jawbone

If a person has a protruding jaw line or jaw hinge, this indicates people who will stop at nothing to achieve what they want, including selling out their friends or family. We also do not like to see knots on the jaw hinge, especially on a person with Peach Blossom eyes, as this indicates they are susceptible to STDs.

Ages 76-99 - The 12 Animals

For the ages of 76-99, the face is divided into the 12 Celestial animal signs, using the nose as the center focal point and the 12 Palaces, as shown in the diagram below. For males, the ages are sequenced counter-clockwise, beginning from the left while for females, it is clockwise, counting from the right.

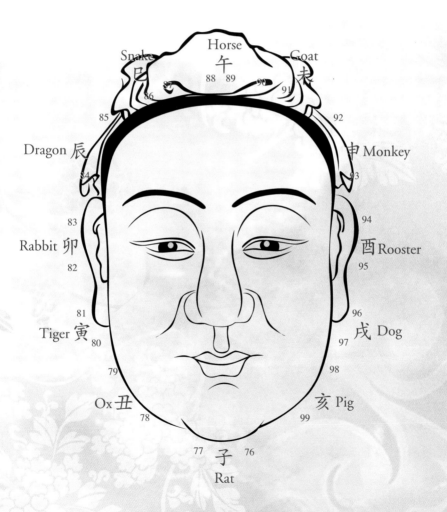

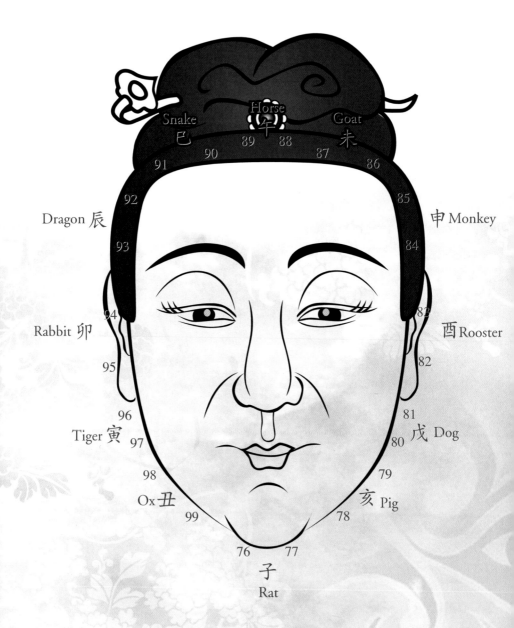

For the ages of 76-99, a person's luck is governed not by a singular position, but by the entire sector. The most important factor when evaluating the fortune of a person over the age of 76 is the quality of the eyes, and not just the age position or sector.

Generally, once a person is of advanced age, we are usually most concerned about health. For those over 76, voice quality, the skin and colour of the forehead, the Qi colour of the skin on the face and of course, the eye spirit are the telling indicators of a person's fortune.

It is rare to have people over 76 come in for face readings but for completeness, I have included the information. Now, you might be wondering, well, what happens if someone aged 100 comes and asks for a face reading? Where do I look?

Once a person reaches the age of 100, the 100 year face map reverts to the first starting position, which is the ears. So if a 100 year old person does ask you for a face reading, check the year 1 position.

In addition to utilising the 100 year map of the face as a reference point, we also utilise the 12 Palaces as a reference point. In the next chapter, we will look at the 12 Palaces of the face and what each of these Palaces mean, and how these 12 Palaces can be utilised for shortcut fast readings of a person's fortune.

Chapter Four:
The Twelve Palaces of the Face

The 12 Palaces are a common theme throughout Chinese Metaphysics. In Purple Star Astrology (Zi Wei Dou Shu 紫微斗數), there are 12 Palaces. In Four Pillars of Destiny (BaZi 八字), there are also 12 Palaces. Western Astrology also uses 12 Houses as a reference point. In Mian Xiang, there are also 12 Palaces.

The 12 Palaces govern the 12 aspects of a person's life.

In earlier chapters, I stressed the importance of always having a point of reference when it comes to reading a person's face. The 12 Palaces is one of the most important techniques of Face Reading because it affords the practitioner with yet another point of reference, besides the 100 year map and the face shape.

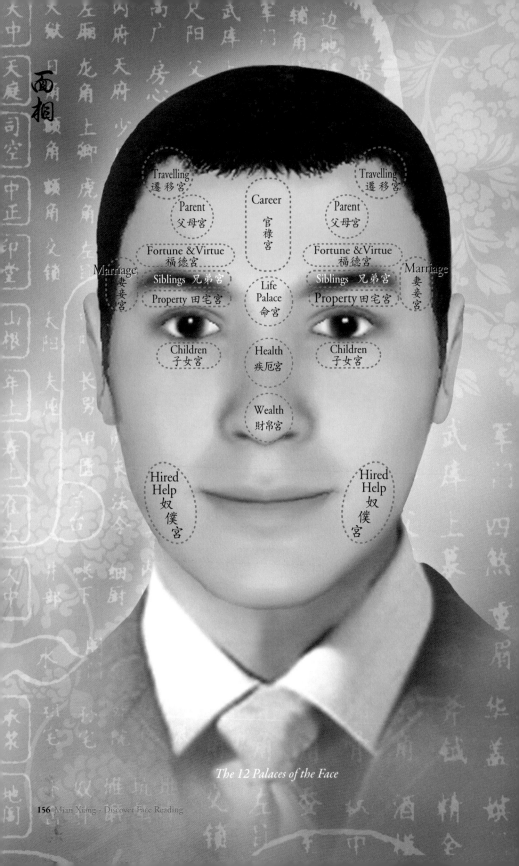

The 12 Palaces of the Face

For example, if some people come up to you and ask about their wealth luck or their luck with siblings, where do you look? Many of my lady clients inquire about husband or marriage luck. If I don't have their BaZi (Destiny) chart, I have their face as a back-up. And by knowing the 12 Palaces, I can immediately focus on the appropriate facial features or area of the face and gain a quick snapshot reading of the person's fortune or luck in that area.

When reading the 12 Palaces, we not only read the features that govern the Palace specifically, but consider other features, in what is known as Multiple Position Reading (Hun Liu Fa 混流法). Where appropriate, I will share with you techniques on how to read certain palaces in tandem with other parts of the face to gain a fuller picture. As your experience grows, you will learn how to handle looking at more than one position. But for now, have fun with the Fixed Position Reading (Ding Liu Fa 定流法) techniques.

The Life Palace 命宮

Every morning when you wake up and look in the mirror to gauge your face for the day, the first palace to look at (or the most important palace to look at if you are in a hurry) is the Life Palace.

This is the most important of the Twelve Palaces because this is a person's House of Life. In face reading, the quality of the Life Palace is of overriding importance. The quality of a person's life – prosperity, intelligence, wealth, health – all depend on the quality of the Life Palace. A bad Life Palace will cancel out any favourable benefits afforded by other good features on the face. It's that important.

Where is the Life Palace located? It is found at the space between your eyebrows, as indicated in the picture below.

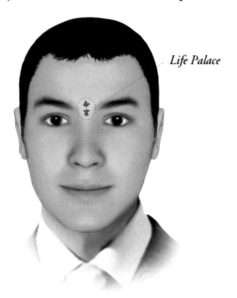

Life Palace

Evaluating the Life Palace:
The Two Finger Rule

How do you determine the quality of your Life Palace? It's easy. The Life Palace should be at least two fingers space in width. Stand in front of a mirror now and check. See if you can place two fingers into the space between your eyebrows.

Two finger space - Life Palace

A tight Life Palace is one where there is only one finger's width in the space between the eyebrows. A broad Life Palace is one where you can fit two fingers comfortably into the space between the eyebrows.

If a person has a tight Life Palace, this indicates the person will have a poor quality of life. What does poor quality of life mean? Now, it does not mean that you will be poor or living below the poverty line. On the contrary, even very wealthy people can have a poor quality of life.

One finger space - Life Palace is tight

Now, you must be wondering – what the heck is Joey talking about? How can someone be rich and have a poor quality of life? What's the point in having all the money in the world but such poor health that you can't enjoy what your money can buy for you? A poor quality of life also means you may be rich, but you don't feel happy or fulfilled.

People with tight Life Palaces often feel troubled, they constantly feel short-changed. Think carefully and you will realise that you probably know someone like this. The high flyer at work who somehow thinks they are not as good as their friends. People who feel that life is always not fair to them even when things have gone their way. People with tight

Life Palaces are usually filled with negativity or pessimism. They are often stressed because they are constantly dissatisfied or unable to stop and smell the roses. A tight Life Palace often also indicates narrow-mindedness.

Tight Life Palace

A broad and fleshy Life Palace, by contrast, belongs to optimistic people who are often able to turn difficult circumstances into positive ones. These people enjoy a good quality of life, even if they are not rich. They see the simple pleasures in life, and live their life to the fullest, even when faced with challenges.

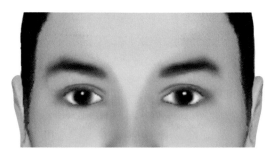

Broad Life Palace

Qualifying the Life Palace

An important qualifier for the Life Palace is that it should be fleshy and with no bones protruding or visibly protruding from it. As the Life Palace is at the same level as the eyebrows, some people have prominent bones underneath the eyebrow that bulge or protrude out. If the Life Palace is not fleshy, then a person has to work very hard and exert significant effort just to achieve a simple matter. Money comes hard and relationships just as hard.

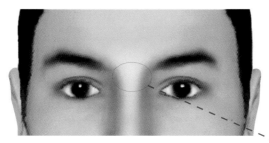

Bony Life Palace

If the Life Palace is broad, fleshy with a fresh colour on the face, it means that goals can be achieved without having to move hell, heaven and earth! Life is smooth and relaxed. People with broad fleshy Life Palaces handle stress better because they are optimistic and always look at the silver lining in the dark cloud. They are open minded and thus, more able to overcome their difficulties or challenges in life.

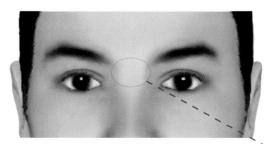

Fleshy Life Palace

Aside from denoting a person's quality of life, the Life Palace also tells us about a person's family life, their relationship with their family and whether or not their home is harmonious. A tight Life Palace indicates a cold family life – the home is lonely and quiet. A broad Life Palace belongs to a person who has good family values and goes home to a family that is warm, caring and harmonious.

Now, like all things, we want moderation. The Life Palace should not be too broad either.

Earlier on, I said that the Life Palace should be 2 fingers in width. What if a person has a Life Palace that is more than 2 fingers in width?

If a Life Palace is broader than 3 fingers width, the person is too generous, is very carefree and cannot weigh the importance of events in his or her life. These are people who can't tell when a situation is serious and requires action, and when a situation is not life and death. They often have poor money management skills and are people who do not value self-improvement or the cultivation of knowledge. Forget about asking these people to a motivational seminar! They would rather spend the afternoon at home sleeping.

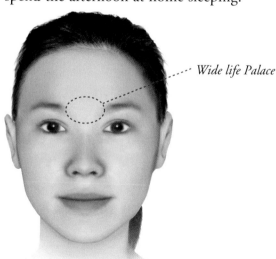

Wide life Palace

Here is a reason not to frown but to smile in life! Frowning actually makes crane's feet or wrinkles appear on your Life Palace (try it in front of a mirror!). The Life Palace should not be too wrinkled. A heavily wrinkled Life Palace indicates a troubled stressful life or a person who is at the crossroads of his or her career or someone who thinks a lot. Crane's feet or wrinkles on the Life Palace also indicate loneliness, meaning the person often feels under pressure, frustrated and not understood by even his or her nearest and dearest.

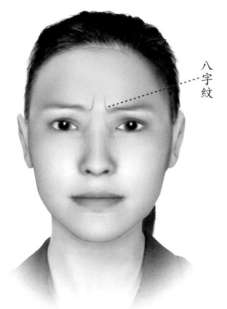

Lines Locking the Life Palace

A line piercing the Life Palace is also not desirable – this is known as the Needle Piercing Through the Heavenly Heart 懸針破印. It usually denotes loneliness in marriage and is particularly bad for married women. A Needle Piercing Through the Heavenly Heart denotes not having a husband – in practical terms, it means you will see your spouse or children infrequently or you will not have much affinity with them. If a man has this line on his Life Palace, he is lonely and is not a family-type man - he spends very little time with his family.

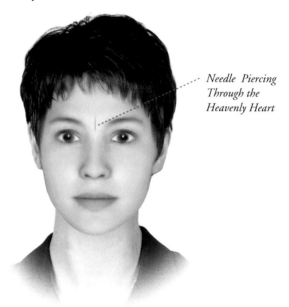

Needle Piercing Through the Heavenly Heart

The Life Palace should not be sunken either – a sunken Life Palace denotes a person who is easily depressed or who is suppressed by other people. This person is often easily depressed and the minute a challenge is thrown at them, becomes quickly de-motivated.

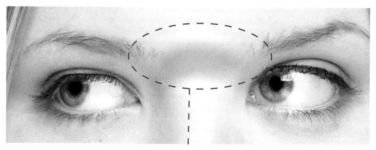

Sunken Life Palace

When evaluating the Life Palace, make sure you also check the eyebrow tips. The hair on the eyebrows should not grow in the direction of the Life Palace but instead, grow in the direction of the hairline. Eyebrows that grow in the direction of the Life Palace indicate individuals with massive egos and often, abilities that do not match what they claim to be able to do. These people suffer from an excess of ambition and often end up experiencing a very severe and significant downfall as a result of over-reaching on their goals.

Eyebrow tip growing towards Life Palace

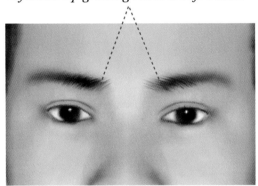

Career Palace 官祿宮

The Career Palace is the entire frontal axis of the forehead spanning positions 15, 19, 22, 25 and 28 on the 100 year map. This entire axis of positions is known as the Career Palace. As the name implies, it tells us about a person's career – the type of work he or she can undertake, the type of job he or she can perform, the types of businesses he or she can flourish in or the type of professional roles he or she can handle.

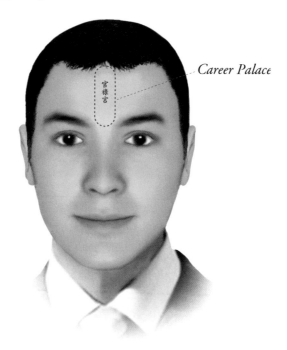

官祿宮

Career Palace

The Career Palace lets us evaluate a person's career luck – it tells us what kind of status and position in life, in society, in a company, a person can achieve. Can a person work in a multi-national corporation or international organisation? Can a person be an entrepreneur? Should a person choose a career in public service? All these are determined by looking at the Career Palace, along with the Wealth Palace.

Often, people find it difficult to tell one forehead from another. Now, Face Reading is an art with lots of nuances and subtleties so you have to learn to look at foreheads under different light and at different angles. At different angles, under different light, even from different distances, you will see dents, bumps, lumps, scars. A side view for example can help you determine whether or not the forehead is tilted forward, bulging or slanting backwards.

The highs and lows of foreheads

Rule number one when it comes to the Career Palace – height is good. The Career Palace should always be high. How do you tell if the forehead is high or not? Look at the hairline to begin with. From the hairline, measure a loose 5 finger space to your Life Palace (which is position 28). Anything less than 5 fingers space, face reading practitioners regard as being a low forehead.

5 Fingers space on Forehead

We want to see a tall palace with no dents. What do I mean when I say no dents? I mean no lumps, no sunken or scars on the Career Palace. It should be tall and smooth.

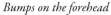

Bumps on the forehead   *Smooth forehead*

A good quality Career Palace is high and tall and broad. Now you might be thinking, sounds a bit like the Life Palace? Yes, the Life Palace and Career Palace go hand in hand – a tight Life Palace usually means the Career Palace is tight and vice versa.

If you have a tall and high forehead, you can be a successful politician or climb up the corporate ladder to the top ranks in a big corporation. Look at figures like Colin Powell, Dr Mahathir, George Bush, Bill Clinton – they all have tall and broad foreheads. Even Arnold Schwarzenagger has a tall forehead, hence his venture into politics. Of course, the success of their political career, the position they can hold (two bit politician, state governor or president of a country) depends on how smooth and well-developed their career palace and the entire forehead is.

The more bumps or unevenness you have, the more obstacles there will be in the climb up the greasy pole of politics. Generally, to be in public service or politics, a tall and squarish forehead is needed. If you just want to be the CEO or director of a large corporation, a moderately high and rounded forehead is acceptable.

Now, a low forehead with a low Career Palace does not mean the person is a dimwit. A low forehead belongs to people who cannot work in multinational companies and who should not contemplate a career in public service or in politics. It also means these people are hands on, not intellectual types. They are better in jobs that do not require too much thinking or intellectual analysis, but physical effort or even, brute force. Usually, these are people who also come out into the job market early in life.

Low forehead

Quick or Slow? Check the Forehead

In performing a career reading based on a person's face, the main thing we are concerned with is giving the person helpful advice and guiding them towards the right kind of career. The forehead not only tells us what kind of career a person can have, but also provides helpful indicators on what kind of job a person can perform.

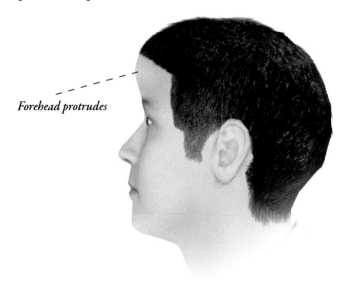

Forehead protrudes

If a person's forehead protrudes, he or she thinks slowly. If his or her forehead protrudes but his or her chin recedes, he or she thinks slowly but acts quickly. This person requires a week to make a decision but he or she acts on his decisions very quickly.

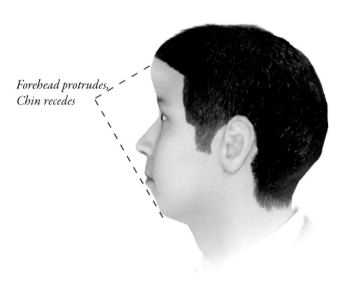

Forehead protrudes,
Chin recedes

If the top of the head protrudes and the chin protrudes, this is the face of a slowpoke – he or she thinks slowly and also takes action like a snail! If the forehead slants backwards, this is a person who thinks quickly but does not always arrive at the right conclusion!

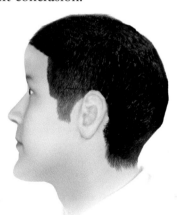

Forehead and chin protrude

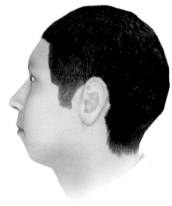

Forehead and chin receding

Once you have established the 'type' of person from the forehead, you can then advice him or her (or prospective employers) how best to utilise the person. If a job requires a person who is quick-witted, then you don't want a slow thinker. Some jobs on the other hand require fast action but perhaps more measured thinking – in which case, you want a person who has a protruding forehead but receding chin! Can you see how useful face reading is?

This knowledge is also particularly useful for people in sales and marketing. Some customers require more thinking time before buying, thus you need to give them space to think and you mustn't push them or you lose the sale. Others are 'impulsive' buyers, they need to be motivated to make the decision on the spot! If you give them time to think about it, they'll lose interest. How do you know which type of customer a person is? Just check their forehead and chin. Impulsive buyers have slanting foreheads and receding chins, while procrastinating customers have protruding forehead and protruding chins.

Now, what about foreheads with bulging veins? This indicates high intelligence only if the bulge is along the Career Palace and not elsewhere. Usually these people may also be spiritual in nature and are usually people who are interested in undergoing religious studies such as going to a seminary or into theology.

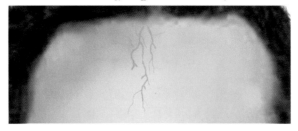

Faint green veins

Parents, you should be careful of injuries to your child's forehead as a scar to the forehead indicates damage to the career. A dent to the Career Palace indicates obstacles and set backs in climbing the corporate ladder.

When you examine your forehead in the mirror, make sure that the flesh is clear and the skin is fresh looking. Dull or dry skin here indicates career problems. A dark patch or Blackish Qi is not good – this indicates that you are going to change jobs or worse, a pink slip is on its way to you.

So what kind of forehead is common in entrepreneurial types or business men? Often, creative and innovative entrepreneurs will have broad and full foreheads. A high forehead is not necessary since not all entrepreneurs after all, go on to be CEOs of their own companies – look at the founders of Yahoo and Google. But a broad full forehead is common with entrepreneurs and businessmen. Most important is a fleshy forehead as this indicates practical skills, the ability to network with helpful people and the presence of friends in high places.

You probably know a few friends off the top of your head who have high and broad foreheads but don't seem to be terribly successful business people or anything but entrepreneurial. So is this face reading stuff inaccurate?

Tall, wide and full forehead

Well, remember that at this stage, you probably can only see what is very obvious on the face so it's possible you have missed a few subtle features, most notably, dents, minor bumps and lines, all which contribute to the quality of the forehead. These features are often very subtle and you need to do a close up to check to see if they are there. The other feature that must be considered in tandem with the forehead are the Wealth Palace and the Life Palace.

The Wealth Palace 財帛宮

Everyone wants to know about money and the fun in Face Reading is that you can almost instantly, once you have learned all the nuances of examining the Wealth Palace, tell who is rich, who is a stingy miser and who is not going to be rich, at one glance. Now, the question is, where should you direct that glance?

At their nose of course! The nose represents the Wealth Palace of a person and when looking at the nose, we are interested in the nose tip, the nose wings, the nostrils and to some degree, the nose bridge.

Now, sometimes in my classes and seminars, people mistake big noses for big wealth. This is not a reason to go out and have your nose enlarged. Yes, a big nose represents big wealth but it has to be in relation to a person's face. You cannot take one person's big nose and put it on a small person's face – it should be big, relative to your own features. Moderation is the key!

A good nose: Charisma is the word

Now, this concept of 'charismatic' is difficult to explain. In Chinese, this term for Charismatic is called 氣勢 Qi Shi.

The best way really to understand and appreciate the meaning of a 'charismatic' nose is really to just go to the bookshop and look at the pictures of very wealthy individuals like Donald Trump, Warren Buffett and Bill Gates. You will very quickly discern at least, what the 'charismatic' nose looks like! But nonetheless, I will endeavour to explain and capture the essence of 'charisma' when it comes to noses in this section.

Let's first consider the shape of the nose. A good nose should not be crooked. It must be thick, broad and strong looking. It should not be bony. It should not hook, it should not be sharp and pointy at the tip.

We also want the nose to be fleshy – not fat, but fleshy. A fleshy nose denotes a pleasant person with few ill-intentions in life.

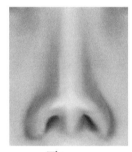

Thin nose

In contrast, people with thin noses are most certainly selfish and harbour ill-intentions or ill-feelings to other people more easily. People with thin noses are often people who think of their own benefits first. A nose that has thin flesh belongs to people who are poor or have no capacity to save money.

The nose tip represents wealth capacity while nose wing represents ability to make money. The tip of the nose should be rounded, denoting high wealth capacity. Look at the nose of Bill Gates or Warren Buffett or Donald Trump – you will notice that their nose tips are pleasantly rounded. Their noses are not fat and clumpy, but slim and elegant, with a perfectly rounded tip. Imagine a cigar stuck on where their nose is – that is what a charismatic nose looks like.

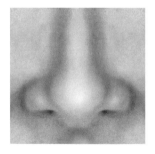

Fleshy and tall nose

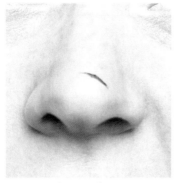

Scar on the nose

The nose must not just have a good shape, but good colour and good texture. It's okay for the skin to be a little shiny, but we don't want an oily nose. We also don't want scars on the nose – this denotes a punctured Wealth Palace. Guess what – when your Wealth Palace is punctured, your wealth leaks out.

Some people have very visible lines on their nose or their nose wings are clearly demarcated by a line, as in the picture below. These tend to be people who have a lot of earning potential but no saving capacity. They are usually frugal people or people who have to be frugal. Sometimes, they are people who are rich, but in debt.

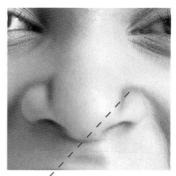

Visible lines locking nostrils

The nostrils must also be taken into consideration when evaluating the nose. Nostrils should not be visible when a person is viewed from the front – visible nostrils (usually due to an upturned nose) indicate a leaking wealth palace. People with exposed nostrils cannot save money, usually because they are spendthrift. A nose with the nostrils that are not seen when viewed from the front indicates a protected Wealth Palace that is strong.

Nostrils seen from front view   *Nostrils can't be seen from front view*

The nose must always be looked at in context of the cheeks. Cheeks that are big and broad can make even a big nose look small or squeezed together.

Cheeks squeezing the nose

A Good Husband Nose?

When I do BaZi reading for ladies, I usually have a glance at their nose before I look at the BaZi chart, especially when one of the questions that the lady client is inquiring about relates to relationships. Why?

You see, a woman's nose also represents her husband. If her nose has a problem, usually her husband or marriage has a problem. A mole or birthmark on the nose for example is not so good for ladies as a mole on the nose indicates not just a health problem but also suggests a possible third party in the marriage.

On the female face, a woman's nose represents her "husband star." To land a good husband, a woman has to have a fleshy nose, with a charismatic nose bridge.

What is a charismatic nose bridge? It is a nose bridge that is moderately high, and not dipping or knotted. A charismatic nose bridge denotes a capable husband.

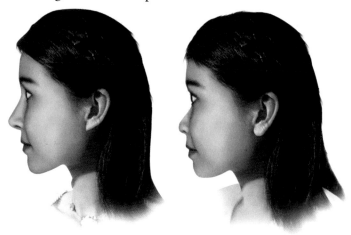

High nose bridge   *Low nose bridge*

Lady with charismatic nose   *Lady with small nose*

Now, it's important, in the Chinese family context, that a woman marries a capable husband who can take care of her. In Chinese society, a woman has Gui Qi 貴氣 when she has a reasonably wealthy, loving husband, who takes good care of her and their family and can give her a leisurely life. Now, what does it take to have Gui Qi or, loosely translated, the aura of elegance? A good nose.

Generally, small noses belong to second wives or mistresses. A woman with a nice fleshy and unbroken non-protruding bridge, with a rounded nose tip and visible nose wings is the one who will end up with a good man who has money. While these ladies are not always exactly supermodel material, they do have the last laugh I'm afraid.

Now, you might be wondering – how did we go from the issue of wealth to the issue of husbands? Remember, your wife's nose (or girlfriend for that matter) reflects on you. If she has a bad nose, it means YOU, her husband, are not all that capable or wealthy. If she has a good nose, it means good luck and good fortunes for you, her husband!

Moral of the nose story: Chose a woman with the right nose (not necessarily a pretty nose) and that means good fortune for you!

The Property Palace 田宅宮

The Property Palace represents your assets, landed property and more importantly, it represents your home. It represents the place that you live in. Do you live in a comfortable home? An expensive luxurious home? Will your house have problems with the plumbing or endless little niggling problems? It is all revealed in the Property Palace.

Like many other features on the face, the Property Palace has to be read in relation to another palace, which is the Wealth Palace – this will let us determine how much property a person can own in his or her lifetime.

The Property Palace is located in-between the eyes and the eyebrows. We like the Property Palace to be broad and well-defined, indicating a good house with no problems and good living conditions.

Property Palace

What the Property Palace Tells Us

A simple reading of the Property Palace can be done like this: if the Property Palace is tight, meaning the space between the eyes and the eyebrows is tight, the person prefers to live in a small house, not a big house. In other words, these are people who can quite happily live in apartments or condos. If the Property Palace is spacious and broad, that means the person likes to live in a big house. These people probably prefer living in landed property, with a large back garden for example.

Tight *Broad*

Tight Property Palace *Broad Property Palace*

Where fine hairs of the eyebrow grow downwards, towards the Property Palace or touching the eyes, this is defined as a low Property Palace. If this feature is found on a man, this is known as the Long Grass Covering the Eyes formation. Now, what happens to long grass? It gets cut. This means that not only do these people have a low Property Palace, but they are constantly hitting a glass ceiling at work or constantly being push down as they climb the career ladder.

Generally, it is not considered good for a man to have a low Property Palace. Low eyebrows, particularly eyebrows that seem to be pressing the eyes, indicate a man who is afraid of his wife or bullied by his wife. Is there an exception to the rule you ask? Yes, there is, if the eyes are slightly sunken in, the eyes are long or the eyes have strong 'eye spirit'.

Eyes suppressed by eyebrows

Dark patches in the area around the eyes and in the Property Palace indicate that the home is not happy and there is a lot of discontent or domestic problems at home.

Sunken or deep set eyes. Dark, patchy property palace.

Health Palace 疾厄宮

The Health Palace spans the center of the bridge of the nose, from positions 44 and 45 on the 100 year map. These two positions combine together to form the Health Palace. The Health Palace does not only relate to your own personal health but the health of those in your home or house.

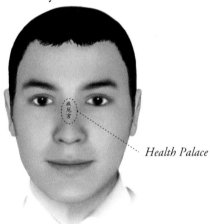

Health Palace

We don't like lines, vertical or horizontal, that cross the Health palace at positions 44 or 45. If there are vertical or horizontal lines across the nose when a person smiles, it indicates constant problems with health. Generally, people with low Mountain Roots (position 41) are more prone to illness than those with high Mountain Roots who generally have more robust health.

line on the Health Palace

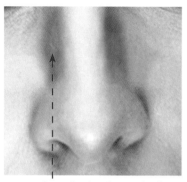

Dark patches beside nose bridge

When looking at the Health Palace, we also are concerned with the nose bridge. When the nose bridge is thin, and there are shadows on the side of the nose, this indicates problems with the back bone. If your nose suddenly has reddish veins or lines appearing on your nose, this suggests a blood related problem. If there is a knot on the nose at the point of the health palace, this indicates that the person has problems with his digestive system.

Mian Xiang practitioners often use what we call Multiple Position Readings to gain an accurate picture of a situation. So for example, when looking at Health issues, if we see a problem with the Health Palace, and also a corresponding dark Travelling Palace and white eyebrows, this indicates a car accident is likely. Sometimes, we will look at the colour or quality of the Qi on the nose. Do you know that different colours of Qi are visible on the face? Dark Qi or Black Qi indicates health problems, especially if it appears on the nose.

Now, discerning Qi colour is not easy and takes a lot of observation and effort. Don't be too concerned if you can't see any Qi colour – focus on what you can see, not what you cannot see when it comes to Face Reading.

Marriage Palace 妻妾宮

In this section I will delve a little bit more into the Marriage Palace for both gentlemen and ladies. The Marriage Palace differs, depending on the gender of the person in question. Now, the old adage is ladies first, so I will talk about the Marriage Palace for women first.

For ladies, the nose doubles up as both the Wealth Palace and the Marriage Palace. The rational for this is quite simple – in the old days, women didn't work. So they got their money from their husbands. Obviously, this is the exception rather than the norm these days but that doesn't mean the principle is not relevant!

To appreciate the quality of a woman's husband, Mian Xiang practitioners look at a lady's husband star. However, being a BaZi consultant, I find Mian Xiang can be very useful, especially when in the consultation, both husband and wife appear but only one is seeking a consultation, as this little story illustrates.

A recent BaZi reading I did was for a gentleman, who came to the consultation with his wife. From his BaZi chart, I could see that this gentleman was a Xin Metal, using Ding Fire, a structure we call 7 Killings Structure in BaZi. It was clear to me that he was very likely engaged in a profession that involved some element of illicit trade but I was hesitant naturally, to say this to the gentleman in the absence of any compelling evidence or statement as such from him.

So, I looked at his wife's nose.

I noticed his wife's nose was slightly crooked. This is usually an indicator that the husband is in what I would put as 'a high risk' business. I carefully asked the gentleman is this was so, and he nodded, saying he was seeking a consultation in order to find a way out.

More commonly of course, a lady comes to see me and wants to know: will I get a good husband? Now that you have this book in your hands, the answer to this question is simple: ask your nose!

A lady's nose is her husband star. Now, to evaluate your own nose (and your future or current husband), you need to be able to see the nose in profile (the side view) and of course, the view from the front.

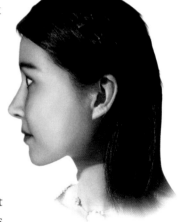

High and charismatic nose bridge

We like the nose bridge to be straight and upright in profile, as this indicates a capable husband who is a professional and leader in his field. If your nose is fleshy, then your husband (or future husband) is likely to be an entrepreneur. A curved nose bridge also indicates a husband who is an entrepreneur.

Now, most ladies generally like to have a pert, small nose but in Mian Xiang, this is not considered a good nose. In the old days, women with small noses and big cheeks were usually second wives. In the modern context, such women are usually mistresses. Of course, this does not mean every woman with a small nose and big cheeks will be a second wife or mistress. Normally, Mian Xiang practitioners like me will advise the lady in question to circumvent any problems by either marrying a divorced gentleman or an older man.

For ladies, a good face is a face that we say 'Wang Fu Yi Zi 旺夫益子'– brings good fortune to the husband and benefits the children. The nose is often an important determining factor in the ability of a woman to have a 'Wang Fu Yi Zi 旺夫益子' life. A fleshy nose, with fleshy nose wings, non exposed nostrils, upright nose bridge when viewed in profile and fleshy cheekbones, normally is the nose of a woman who will bring good fortune to her husband. In Mian Xiang, such a face is also known as the appearance of a boss lady or Lao Pan Niang 老板娘, someone who can be the wife of a big boss.

*Fleshy **nose**, high bridge,*
fleshy nostril wings

So what about the guys then? How do you evaluate a man's Marriage Palace? The Marriage Palace for a male is called the Jian Men 奸門 and is located just a finger space away from the eye (see picture below). This is also known as the Wife Palace.

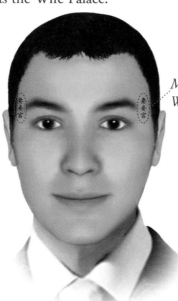

Marriage Palace /
Wife Palace

Now, we like this position to be slightly fleshy and most importantly, not sunken in. A sunken Marriage Palace indicates an unhappy and dissatisfying relationship with the wife.

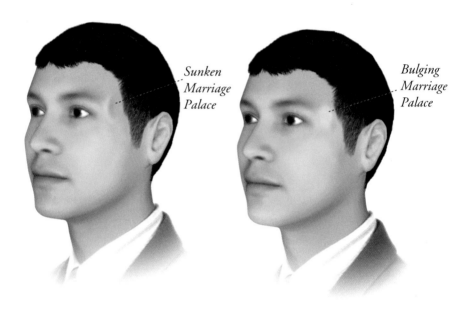

Sunken Marriage Palace

Bulging Marriage Palace

Of course, we don't want this Palace to be excessively fleshy or bulging either, unless of course, you happen to like being bossed at home or have a tigress for a wife. Usually, men with fleshy or bulging temples will find that, like it or not, they will be attracted to (and marry) a bossy lady.

When we look at the male Marriage Palace, we are usually looking for Peach Blossom lines. What are Peach Blossom lines? These are known in Western terms as crow's feet, those little lines that emerge from the eyes when a person smiles. Have you seen when a man smiles and his eyes crinkle up? Peach Blossom lines are those crinkles. They are also known as Fish Tails.

Men with Fish Tails or Peach Blossom lines are usually flamboyant, suave and smooth. The kind of men who have the ability to sweet talk ladies and sweep them off their feet, like Clark Gable in Gone with the Wind. Now, this charm does not mean that they have bad marriages or are philanderers. It simply means they enjoy the attention of ladies generally.

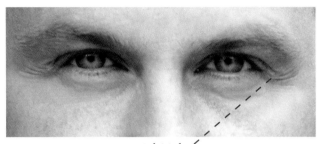

Fish Tails

Peach Blossom lines are only a cause for concern when they grow downwards or are too long and cut into the Marriage Palace. This indicates the man's flirtatious activities often lead to dangerous liaisons and that there is a strong likelihood of divorce due to extra-marital affairs.

What do we mean by the line cuts into the marriage palace? Look at the picture below.

Fish Tails cutting into the marriage palace

Sometimes, Peach Blossom lines are coupled with a bulging Spouse Palace. This indicates a man who strays because his 'home tigress' is fierce or has a strong character, hence, the tendency to go out and look for fun.

When a gentleman comes in for a professional consultation and inquires on the issue of marriage, we not just look at the lines on the Marriage Palace, but whether there are red lines or darkish Qi, which suggest potential separation or very serious, marital-threatening arguments.

Children Palace 子女宫

The Children Palace is directly under the eyes, in the eyebags. This Palace represents your children and your relationship with your children. Do you have a good relationship with your children? Will your children be filial to you? It all depends on the quality of this palace.

Children Palace

What are we looking for when it comes to the Children Palace? We like the eyebags to have a clear colour, the skin is vibrant and there are no crinkles. This denotes good children affinity.

If the Children Palace is fleshy, meaning not swollen or puffy but nicely fleshy and not dark, and the person does not have sunken eyeballs (or eyebrows that protrude out), this means the person's children are capable people, who will bring good name to their family with their deeds. They are capable, helpful and not wastrels.

A lot of times, when I meet a parent who has a disabled child, the eyebags usually have dark lines or dark patches. These appear irrespective of whether or not a person has had enough sleep. Many people think that dark circles under the eyes only appear if a person has not had enough sleep but this is not the case – parents with children who are disabled or mentally disabled or children who will be dependant on you for life will have these darkened eyebags. Sometimes, dark eyebags appear on parents who are overly-worried or paranoid about their children, especially mothers.

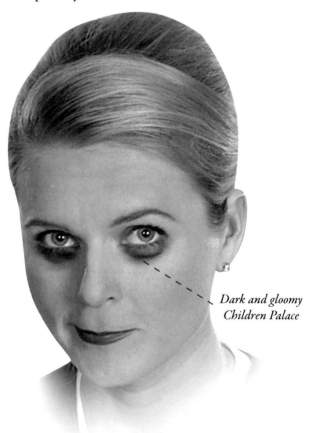

*Dark and gloomy
Children Palace*

Moms, keep a close watch on your own eyebags to know how your kids are doing overseas. If you have a dark patch just on one eyebag, then this denotes a temporary passing problem with one of your children. Which child? If it is a dark patch on the right, you are worried about your daughter. If it is a dark patch on the left, your son is the cause for concern. If white patches appear on your eyebag, this denotes possible danger to your children.

Generally, we don't like to see any lines running across the eyebags, like in the illustration below. Dark eyebags, coupled with a line running across the eyebag indicates a poor affinity with children or children who are wastrels and inept.

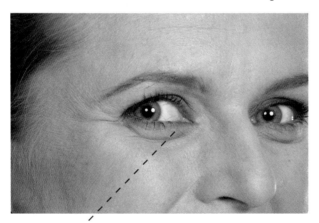

Lines running across Children Palace

Hired Help Palace 奴僕宮

Now, as the name implies, the Hired Help Palace relates to your hired help. From your maid and gardener, to your bodyguard and accountant, this is the Palace that governs your relationship with those who 'help' you in life. The Hired Help Palace is located at the position 74 and 75 in the 100 year map, at the bottom of the jaws. When reading the Hired Help Palace, the chin must always be considered.

Hired Help Palace

Now, in the old days, the Hired Help Palace almost always related to whether or not those people had servants to serve them in their old age. Chinese culture considers it extremely important to have not only hired help, but also, help from family members and friends, in their lifetime.

The Hired Help Palace should not have wrinkles that cross the Palace. This indicates a broken structure and denotes problems with employees or servants or people who work for you. Now, I must dispel this belief that all people have wrinkles when they age. Take a good look at Queen Elizabeth II, Li Ka Shing or Warren Buffett – they are advanced in age but they do not have a lot of wrinkles on their faces!

It's all in the Chin

The Hired Help Palace should be broad and fleshy. There should be a spacious area between the mouth and the chin line. This denotes a strong Hired Help Palace, indicating in your lifetime, there will be not just good staff at work, but friends and relatives to help you during your old age. The jawline should be rounded for ladies and gently squarish for men to qualify as a good Hired Help Palace.

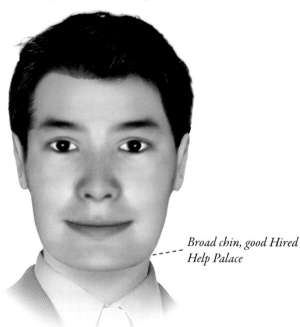

Broad chin, good Hired Help Palace

We also don't want a tight space between the mouth and the chin but a generous space here. It should be fleshy, and not bony, denoting a prosperous and leisurely old age. A bony chin area denotes a miserable old age.

Narrow chin, bad Hired Help Palace

Parents Palace 父母宮

This is located at positions 17 and 18 on the 100 year map, and is also known as the Sun and Moon position. The Sun represents the Father, whilst the Moon represents the Mother. These two positions represent a person's relationship with his parents and is also the Palace to be examined when we are evaluating the health of a person's parents at a certain time.

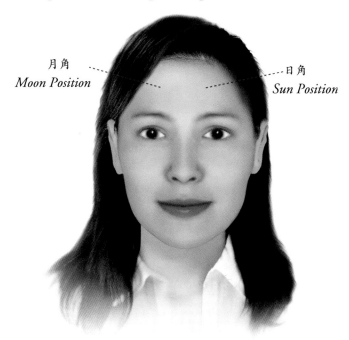

月角
Moon Position

日角
Sun Position

If there are scars protrusions or dents in the Parents Palace, this denotes the person's father passed on early in his life. A dented Sun denotes that a person will not receive help from his father in his lifetime. Similarly, a dented Moon denotes that no help or assistance from the mother. If the forehead is slanted, caused by the Sun and Moon being high and low or not level with each other, this denotes that the person's parents have a poor relationship with each other – the father may have two wives for example or the mother has a lover.

The hairline can also tell us about a person's relationship with his or her parents. A saw hairline, one where there is fine babyhair or tendrils hanging over the hairline, indicates the person brings bad luck to his or her parents.

--- *Sawed-hairline*

Now, what do I mean by bad luck to the parents? This does not mean literally bad luck. In Chinese culture, a person brings bad luck to his or her parents if he or she doesn't get along with his or her parents or particularly, if the relationship with the father is not good. Bad luck here means, parent and child are always in disagreement – they say one, you say two – or cannot see eye to eye.

Lines across the forehead indicate a tough or even miserable life before 30 and unsupportive parents who do not give you a good head start in life. A low and tight forehead that squeezes the Sun and Moon positions together denotes a person who has to stop schooling early in life to help his or her parents or work for his or her parents.

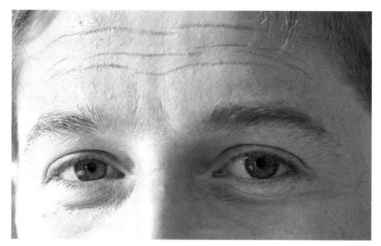

Lines running across the forehead

Siblings Palace 兄弟宫

The Siblings Palace represents your relationship with your siblings. It also reveals the quality of your siblings and characteristics of your siblings. By looking at a person's siblings, we can tell whether or not a person's siblings are in good health and whether or not they are helpful to a person.

Your Siblings Palace is located on the eyebrows and when evaluating the Sibling Palace, we are looking at the length of the eyebrows, the direction of hair growth on the eyebrows and the thickness or density of the eyebrows amongst other things.

Siblings Palace

The quickest and fastest way to make use of the Siblings Palace is to tell if a person comes from a large family or a small family. Now, it is quite a common inquiry at Asian family functions for people to ask how many siblings you have so that is why, this is a useful little face reading trick! You can tell without asking.

Normally, eyebrows that are longer than the eyes denote a person with four or more siblings. If the length of the eyebrows is the same or shorter than the eyes, then the person has less than 4 siblings. See how easy it is?

Having siblings is one thing but helpful siblings are of course, the best kind, especially if you also have a good relationship with them. People who have helpful siblings and who enjoy a good relationship with their siblings have eyebrows that are moderate in density and have eyebrow hair that grows in a uniform direction.

Eyebrows growing in a smooth direction

What about bad relationships between brothers and sisters? You need to look at the eyebrow hair and how it grows. If the eyebrow hair grows in opposing directions (meaning, some grows towards the right, some grows towards the left), this denotes animosity between the siblings in very severe instances or in mild instances, the siblings do not get along. Dense eyebrows denote a patchy relationship between siblings – it is sometimes good, sometimes bad, sometimes just amicable.

Eyebrows growing in a confusing direction (criss crossing manner)

The eyebrows can also be used to gain insight into the health of a person's siblings. A chip or break in the eyebrow denotes a health condition or heart problem or in severe instances, indicates life threatening danger. If the chip or break in the eyebrow is on the right side, this means it is the female sibling that may have a problem. If it is the left side, it means a male sibling may be facing the health difficulty or dangerous situation.

Chip on eyebrow

Eyebrows are also very revealing when it comes to family relationships. How do you know if a person has a stepmother or stepfather or half-brothers and half-sisters? Yin Yang eyebrows – eyebrows where one eyebrow is high and one eyebrow is low when viewed from the front, are highly suggestive of a person who has siblings from different mothers or different fathers. To get confirmation, check the Parents Palace and the ears. If the ears are set at different levels (one high, one low), that is further confirmation that the person has half-siblings.

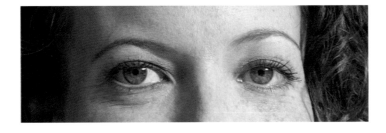

One eyebrow higher than the other

Travelling Palace 遷移宮

The Travelling Palace is where a person's Sky Horse resides and represents travel and mobility. It is located at position 23 and 24 on the 100 year map – this is the left and right corners of the forehead.

Travelling Palace

The Travelling Palace determines if a person can migrate successfully or whether or not an overseas job posting will lead to success. A spacious Travelling Palace with fresh colour indicates a person who can migrate and successfully begin a new life in a new country.

For quick readings, this Palace will tell us whether or not a person will have success in business on an overseas trip. You see, Face Reading can also be used for quick readings on luck of a certain day by looking at the Qi colour, the texture and freshness of the face at those positions. A person with a dark coloured Travelling Palace is likely to encounter bad fortune during travel (losing documents, encountering obstacles during travel) or who will find the trip does not produce much results.

A Travelling Palace that is high and fleshy indicates individuals who must make their money through travelling or businesses that are highly mobile in nature. Alternatively, they are involved in businesses that require constant evolution, are fast paced or in constant flux.

If the Travelling Palace is low, then the person most likely is more suited to a steadier job that involves little movement or travel. These are individuals who are best suited for office bound jobs.

High Travelling Palace

Low Travelling Palace

Fortune and Virtue Palace 福德宮

The Fortune and Virtue Palace is located above your eyebrows, just above the bone, as indicated in the picture below.

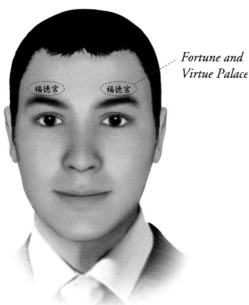

Fortune and Virtue Palace

We have to be a bit careful with the words Fortune and Virtue – these do not literally refer to your money and 'chastity' as it were. Rather, the Fortune and Virtue Palace relates to perceptions of life, mental happiness and overall, a person's view on his or her life as it were. The Fortune and Virtue Palace must always be read together with a person's chin and eyes. Why? Because to have a good quality of life, a person's heart, as represented by his eyes, must be happy. The Chin relates to the ability to enjoy life and so a good chin denotes a person who can enjoy the simple and sophisticated pleasures of life.

The Fortune and Virtues Palace should be fleshy, denoting a person who has a positive optimistic outlook and many friends and happy friendships. This person is able to find fulfilment in life. There should be no vertical or horizontal lines cutting the Fortune and Virtues Palace or the person will find it difficult to be happy and contented.

If the Fortune and Virtue Palace has protruding bones, these are people who are hard and demanding of themselves. Their opinion is strong and their life is not contented because they are in constant pursuit of perfection.

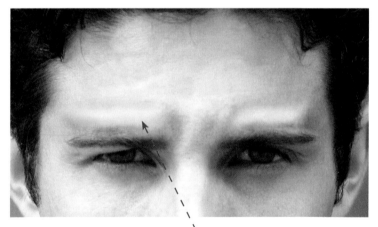

Protruding bones in the Fortune and Virtue Palace

A Fortune and Virtue Palace that is cut by lines denotes people of infirm morals or who do not have firm principles. They can easily be persuaded to 'reconsider their position'. This is especially so if the person has weak eyes – eyes that are lifeless and not alert.

Lines piercing into the Fortune and Virtue Palace

The eyebrows should not pierce into the Fortune and Virtue Palace, as illustrated by the image above. This denotes a person who is hasty, to the point where his or her decisions are acted upon too swiftly and without thorough consideration.

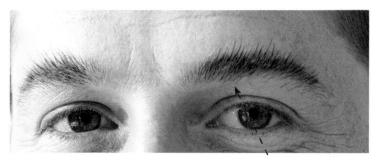

Upward piercing eyebrows, piercing into the Fortune and Virtue Palace

Now, the Fortune and Virtue palace also relates to a person's friendship with others and their perception of the friendship. People with scars or lines across their Fortune and Virtue Palace often have complex or difficult friendships – they are people who are your friend one day, your enemy the next day. Or, they are people who suffer from many friendships that have gone sour. People with scars or lines across their Fortune and Virtue Palace also find it difficult to make friends, often because they have very strong or over-riding opinions.

With the knowledge you have from the 100 year map and the 12 Palaces, you will already have plenty of information With the knowledge you have from the 100 year map and the 12 Palaces, you will already have plentry of information and techniques to read and discover a lot about the people around you. But, the 12 Palaces are not the be all and end all of Face Reading.

The 12 Palaces have in fact much broader context and meanings, but of course, since we are on a beginner's text, I've restricted the context and meanings to keep them simple and easy to understand and learn. For example, the Siblings Palace, which is represented by the eyebrows, also relates to a person's character and nature: is the person strong-willed or gutless? Righteous or slimy? The nose for example, doesn't just relate to Wealth but also relates to a person's integrity and self-belief.

Just remember, as you go on to the other chapters, that we're just scratching the tip of the iceberg!

Chapter Five:
Do Moles Have Meanings?

People love to ask about moles at my public talks and seminars. I guess this is because moles are easy and obvious features that almost everyone either has or has seen on someone's face.

Do moles have meanings? Yes they do. And there's absolutely nothing complex about moles – all you have to do is be familiar with the 100 year map and the 12 Palaces of the face. You see, a mole on the face will exert an effect based on its position so you just need to know what the position relates to in order to understand what the mole means.

I used to think that this business of moles being bad luck was silly, early in my study of Chinese Metaphysics. I frequently would say to my teacher: hey what can a silly little mole do to you? How bad can it be? I was always very inquisitive but also, liked to ask why and challenge what I was told.

Naturally, my Si Fu decided to undertake a live demonstration for me, telling me about certain events that took place in my life, and all because there was a mole on my face at the point in time. Even then I was not too persuaded. It was only when I began to practice face reading that I realised how the simple mole can tell a lot about a person!

Reading moles is a very easy to learn technique – it helped start me off in the practice of Mian Xiang. And as you read through this chapter, you'll also see, as I did, that moles are a great way to get into face reading and also, plenty of fun!

But before I begin telling you about moles, you have to be able to distinguish between a mole (Mo 墨) and a birthmark (Zhi 痣).

A mole is a small, dark, sometimes protruding growth on the human skin. It is usually black. It sometimes will have fine hair growing out of it. A birthmark or a black mark does not have hair growing out of it and does not protrude. It is usually brown or a lighter black colour.

A mole is a greater cause for concerned compared to a birthmark. It is said in the ancient classics, *Mian Shang Mei Hau Mo* 面上沒好墨 – the face has no good mole. In general, all moles are unfavourable and hence it is quite safe to have them removed. It is only in very exceptional cases that a mole brings or denotes good fortune. Even then, the good fortune will only relate to luck at that particular age. Later on, it will still exert a negative impact over the person's overall luck.

A mole is seen as a 'blockage' of luck or Qi flow. Now, a simple way of reading or evaluating a mole is just to identify which age position the mole is located at or which of the 12 Palaces it is located in, and we can say that at that age, the person will encounter difficulties. So for example, if a person has a mole at the age position of 45, it denotes a Qi blockage at that age and difficulties at that age.

It's that easy!

The reason behind this is that moles represent a 'blockage' of the luck. Thus, a mole in the age position of 45 denotes a blockage of Qi at that age. Meaning, the person is likely to encounter difficulties at that age.

Birthmarks or marks on the face on the other hand are iffy – depending on position and size, they may not be a problem. In rare circumstances, it may even denote good fortune. Why is this so? Because birthmarks most of the time are a 'colouration' of the skin. They usually do not have a protruding surface. No protrusion means no 'blockage' of Qi.

In this chapter, I will talk about some of the more easily recognisable moles and marks. Moles usually are viewed in a situational context and I have taken the liberty of coining names for these moles, largely to help you learn them and at the same time, remember what they mean. Also take note of when I specifically refer to moles and when I refer to marks.

In Face Reading, most moles are considered negative features on the face. I will first share with you some of the bad moles and then I will share with you some exceptions to this rule.

The Stolen Spouse Mole (橫刀奪愛)

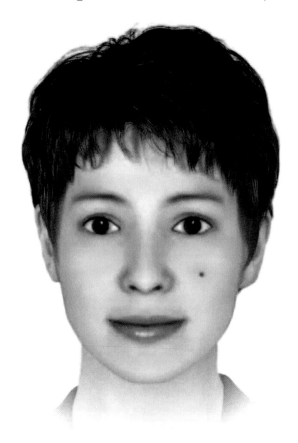

Mole on the left cheek

Have you heard of people who after being in a relationship for the longest time and on the verge of marriage, suddenly lose their significant other to a third party? They probably have the Stolen Spouse Mole. This mole is located directly in the center of the cheek and may be found on either the right or the left cheek.

To qualify as a Stolen Spouse Mole, the mole must be located on the cheek, positioned directly below the eyes.

The presence of this mole indicates that a person will have their boyfriend, girlfriend or spouse snatched from under their nose. Or, in the case of a love triangle, the person with the Stolen Spouse Mole will be the losing party.

Why does a mole on the cheek have this effect? The cheeks, as I have indicated in previous chapters, represent Power. A mole directly on your cheek represents a removal of power and authority in a relationship. What happens when you lose the authority or power to command respect from your spouse? You lose your spouse's interest in you. Or worse, you lose your influence and love to a 3rd party!

A Stolen Spouse Mole is a cause for concern particularly when it is coupled with a thin line across the Marriage Palace at position 41, which suggests adultery, or if a man has particularly thick eyebrows, which suggest the possibility of a friend or best friend becoming a third party in the relationship.

A Stolen Spouse Mole, besides indicating loss of your spouse to someone you know, also indicates the possibility of losing control or authority over something you own. For instance, being forced out of your job or forced out of your own business by your business associates. I've seen many people with this feature; one clear example I remember is a self-made business man who upon taking his company public, ended up, very sadly, being forced out of his own company by the shareholders.

The Counter The Husband Mole

Mole on Position 19

If the mole appears directly at position 19 on the forehead, this counters 'Officer Luck' or luck with husbands for women. This means the woman's marriage is negatively affected – the woman may be mistreated by her husband or have an unhappy marriage.

Position 19 is part of the central axis of the Career Palace. For ladies only, the Career Palace also influences the quality of her spouse. A mole on this position indicates possibility of a third party influence that causes disruption to the happiness in her marriage.

For men who have a mole in this position, this is known as the Counter The Career Mole. A mole here indicates a person's career is stuck or reaches a plateau at an early age. This person either keeps hitting a glass ceiling or he has superiors who simply refuse to let him move up the ladder. A man with a mole at this position will have to wait till his thirties to enjoy good luck and he should not become a politician as he will be unsuccessful.

The Bad Health Mole

Mole on the nose bridge

This is a mole that is found directly on the Health Palace. A mole here indicates that the Qi in the Health Palace is being blocked, denoting a life that is bogged down by lingering illness or long term illness. People with a mole at this position usually suffer from poor blood circulation or stomach/gastrointestinal problems. They are also the first people to get sick should a common flu bug be circulating!

The Crying Mole

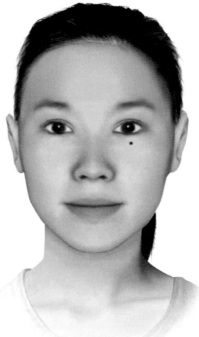

Mole on the eyebag

The Crying Mole is located directly on the eyebags. This mole denotes constant emotional setbacks and for ladies, it represents heartache when it comes to relationships or children. People with this mole are easily moved to tears, be it as a result of their own emotional problems or just the weekly soap opera. This is a very unique mole in that it is a pairing mole – this means that if there is a mole on the eyebag at this position on the right, there will also be a corresponding mole on the right side of the chest, and vice versa with a mole on the left eyebag.

The Crying Mole often appears on the face of people who are usually or easily bogged down by emotional issues. They are often worried and in bad case, paranoid over often trivial matters.

The Limb Breaking Mole

Mole on the Fa Ling

The Limb Breaking Mole is a mole located on the Fa Ling or Laughter Lines. A mole on the left side indicates a broken left leg for a man, the left hand for lady. A mole on the right side will denote a broken right leg for the man, broken right hand for the lady. It may also denote an injury to this area.

Individuals with this mole also face constant challenge when it comes to acquiring recognition in their professional work or in society. This is because the Fa Ling or Laughter Lines indicate respect and honour from others. When this line is blocked by a mole, the ability to command respect is greatly diminished.

The Busybody Mole

Ever met someone who is really nosy? Well next time you do, check out if he or she has this mole on the chin.

Mole on the chin

This mole denotes an inquisitive nature – think of the aunt who is always curious to know every little detail about your personal life – the busybody. This mole is located at near the chin and on the right or left side of the chin. The size of the mole determines just how annoying the person will be: a small mole and the person will be moderately inquisitive, a large mole denotes a person who asks too many questions.

Their inquisitive nosy nature will be worse if the mole is large and has hair growing out of it! These are often pretty imaginative people too, which no doubt explains why they are busybodies! Take note though that even though this is a busybody mole, it does have some beneficial effects similar to that of the Eating God Mark. Also, if this mole is not large and is of a healthy colour, it actually denotes the person, though inquisitive, is very intelligent and wise, constantly seeking answers and improvements in life.

The Thief Mole

Ever wondered how to tell if someone is going to be constantly plagued by robbery and theft problems? Or if they are likely to be constantly losing things? Check for the Thief mole.

Mole on the eye tip

This mole is found on the tip of the Property Palace, above the eye, and in the ancient classics, this is referred to as The Thief Outside Your House. A man with a mole at this position on the left side will experience a robbery in his own house or his parents' house. If the mole is on the right eye tip, it is the wife's side of the family that will be plagued by a robbery. People with this mole also find they lose or misplace items easily.

The Psychotic Mole

Weird? Eccentric? Odd? These are the words we often use to describe people who behave without regard for the conventions of society or are outlandish in their manner. Sometimes, they seem to live in a world of their own.

Mole on the Life Gate

This mole is located just in front of the ear, at the Life Gate. In Chinese Face Reading, the Life Gate is the transition point of all the neuro-points in the body. When it is blocked by something such as a large mole, the person may be a little bit eccentric or in severe cases, psychologically disturbed, especially so if the eyes look dull and the forehead is low.

The Lawsuit Mole

Is there a face that constantly attracts legal problems and issues? Well, yes! It is stated in the ancient classics "Jian Men You Zhi Guan Fei Wang 奸門有痣官非旺", meaning "When There is a Mole on the Gan Men, Legal Hassles will be abound".

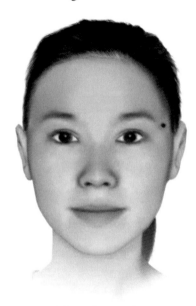

Mole on the temple

This mole is located at the Jian Men 奸門 position, which is also the Spouse Palace for men.

A mole here indicates endless legal problems or hassles caused by backbiters throughout the person's life. This person will often find that he or she is constantly at the center of controversy, rumours or somehow seems to always be the target of backstabbing. The extent of the problem will of course depend on the size of the mole or mark. If it is small and faint, then the problems are irritating but not significant. If it is large, then this person can expect it to involve lawyers and writs flying left and right.

The Wealth Dispersing Mole

Once an elderly lady came to me and asked me, 'Joey, my son keeps spending all of my money, is there a feature on his face that indicates this?' I said 'Yes, and this is how you see it...'

Mole on the nose

The Wealth Dispersing Mole is located on the nose or nose wing and is regarded as a hole in the storage of wealth. This is because the nose is the Wealth Palace and a mole here indicates a leakage in the wealth storage or a wealth-related problem. As you would expect from a leaking wealth storage, people with moles or marks on this spot just cannot save money or just keep losing money. If the mole or mark is very large, it can denote lifelong financial problems for the person. Do not be misled by the presence of the word Wealth here. This is not a good mole.

The Burden Mole

If you are often bogged by the problems of other people, or shouldering massive responsibilities that somehow seem to add 30Kgs of psychological weight, then you probably have the Burden Mole.

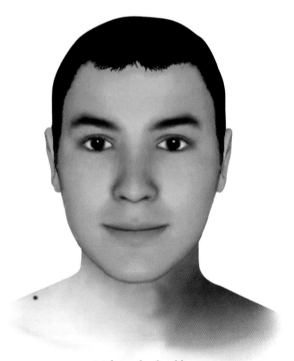

Mole on the shoulder

If you have a mole anywhere along your shoulder, this is known as a Burden Mole. What does the Burden Mole signify? It denotes that the person will have to carry burdens from his family throughout his life. If the mole is on your left shoulder, it is the burdens from male relatives that you must bear. If it is on your right shoulder, it is burdens from female relatives, such as your mother or your sister that you are stuck with.

Remember the phrase from the ancient classics I told you about earlier? *Mian Shang Mei Hau Mo* 面上沒好墨 – translated, it means, the face has no good moles.

Accordingly, most moles are not good to have. Of course, with all things, there are exceptions. There are a few moles that are considered good - I have listed a few here. Generally, it is better if any marks on the face are birthmarks or spots rather than moles and again, I have also selected a few examples of good birthmarks or spots.

The Treasure In The Forest Mole

Ever wondered if you are gifted or are destined to be somebody great? Or perhaps you have a talent and are wondering if one day you will finally have the chance to realise this talent and become famous and rich? Well, check if you have this mole.

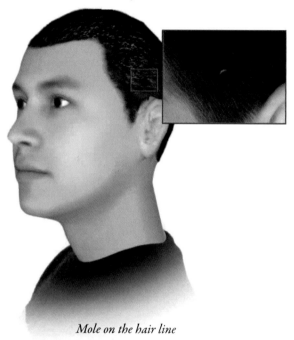

Mole on the hair line

This mole is located inside the hair line, above the ear, on either side of the head. This mole cannot be seen because it is covered by the hairline but if you look carefully, it can be discerned. It is called the 'Treasure in the Forest' in the ancient classics because it denotes a unique potential or talent that once awakened or brought forth, will bring substantial wealth or fame to the person. Why "forest"? Hair in study of Face Reading is represented by the element of Wood. Since we have more than one strand of hair on our heads, that's why it's called a "forest".

The Eating God Mark

Some people seem to know how to enjoy life through good food all the time! Everywhere they go, they find and enjoy good food. And these people sometimes even get to enjoy good food at other people's expense. They get to eat, and guess what, most of the time they don't even have to pay for it. Why? Perhaps they have the Eating God Mark.

Mole on the tip of the lip

The Eating God Mark is located above the corner of the upper lip. This denotes a person who enjoys epicurean experiences throughout his life and will be able to appreciate the finer things in life, from opera to food to art to wine and women. To qualify as an Eating God mark, it must not be a mole that is dark and thick but should be a birthmark or a spot.

The Filial Mole

Parents often ask me, how can we tell if our children will be grateful and filial? How can we tell if our children will take care of (and still be with) us when we grow old and sick in future? Then you need to look for the Filial Mole.

Mole behind the ear

This mole is located on the back of the ear. People with moles on the back of their ear will be filial, take good care of their parents and elders and will listen to their parents. If your child has a mole like this, you can be sure that you won't be in an old folks home in your old age.

The Money Saving Mole

We've discussed the mole that causes a person to lose wealth quickly. But there's one that helps people do just the opposite – that's to save money! People who have this mole usually have nest eggs of a substantial size or have saved up for that rainy day.

Mole underneath nostril

If you have a mole just underneath or next to your nostril, do not remove this! It is the security guard protecting your wealth storage from leaking. A person with this mole not only saves money, but can also attract wealth easily. Hence, it is also known as an absorbing prosperity mole.

The Pearl In The Grass Mark

Often we meet people who seem so talented and yet they seem to be stuck, lacking opportunities to excel or show their talents to the world. Will these people ever be recognised? Well, it depends on whether or not they have a pearl in the grass mark.

Mole in the eyebrow

A spot or mark inside the eyebrow is called 'the pearl in the grass' in the ancient classics. This denotes the presence of a treasure but it is covered by long grass. It indicates a strong determined character with the ability to persevere at something and after much effort, the pearl will emerge, and this person's talent will be recognised. The only drawback to having this spot or mark is there is water-related danger – hence, a person with this mark may always be scalded by hot water or slip on water or in serious cases, may drown.

IQ Mark

Are there any quick, easy and near instant way to tell if a person is smart? Yes of course, look for the IQ Mark on their ears.

Mole on the Ear Ridge / Lobe

This is a mark located on the lobe of the ear or on the ridge of the ears that is visible. This mark denotes a person with high intelligence. A person with this mark will normally do well in exams. This reading does not apply however if it is a mole that is located in this position.

The Twin Mark

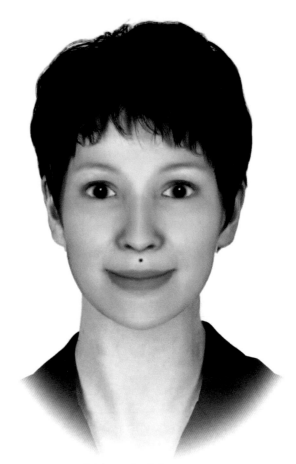

Mole on the philtrum

If there is a small, dot-like mark on the philtrum, this denotes the person will possibly give birth to twins. However if it is a mole, this denotes difficulty giving birth as the philtrum is blocked, representing blockage of the reproductive organs.

The Fu Luk Sau Moles

Fu 福 (Properity), Lu 祿 (Wealth) and Shou 壽 (Longevity) – three important qualities most people will not mind having a bit more of in their lives. Can someone really have it all? To have prosperity, to enjoy abundance in wealth and more importantly, to live a long and healthy life? Yes they can, but only if they have this truly unique and special formation of moles on their body!

If you have three moles, running from the top of the vertebrae all the way down the backbone, to the backside, this is called the Fu Luk Sau mole, representing prosperity, happiness and longevity. This is a good mole formation but rarely seen.

Of course, there are 100 positions on the face so this is by no means an extensive chapter on moles. And people have moles in many places (not just the face!) but for economy of space, I have chosen some of the more common moles to feature.

In the next chapter, we are going to take Face Reading to the practical level, with some techniques which I know will be useful to you on a day to day basis, and in daily business activities.

Chapter Six:
Faces will never be the same again -
Face Reading Applications

All the fun in Face Reading only really starts when you get out on the street (or go to lunch with your friends) and start putting into practice what you have learnt in this book.

Believe me, you will see things in your friends, family members and even the waiter at the restaurant's face, that you never saw before. You may be so busy having fun reading faces that you forget you are having a conversation with someone!

The key to a good start when it comes to the practical application of Face Reading is a good familiarity with the 100 positions of the face and the 12 Palaces. This is because Face Reading is in essence, interpretation of the 100 positions, together with the 12 Palaces.

You also need to exercise a little logical discipline at the same time. Remember, you cannot run before you can walk. Don't try to read the entire face – instead, focus on the key areas and always think about what you are trying to find out about the person, the context of the reading.

In BaZi (Destiny Analysis), I always remind my students that they must always remember the key point of reference during their analysis and reading of a Destiny Chart. In BaZi, the key point of reference is the Day Master.

In Face Reading, deciding what you are trying to read from the person's face is crucial. Is it about relationships? Or about current luck? Perhaps it is a spot on their face or a pimple? Once you have established this, it is then easy for you to decide which of the 100 positions or 12 Palaces you need to consider and evaluate. Then, you can move to the lines and scars, moles, indentations, bumps or bulges and complexion colour in the relevant position or palace that you need to examine.

Yes, that is the 'secret' art of Face Reading!

So, now that we know the technique, let's find out how to go about doing some practical readings!

The Look of Love

On the top ten list of questions (after wealth of course) for both male and females is relationships. During my public talks and seminars on face reading, I am sure to have several questions on relationships.

So where does one start when asked about relationships?

Why, the Marriage Palace of course! If you're not sure where the Marriage Palace is located, flip back to Chapter Four for a quick refresher.

Now, the Marriage Palace differs in location depending on whether it is a lady or a gentleman who is asking the question. A lady's Marriage Palace is her nose so naturally, the first thing you do (without trying to be too rude) is look at her nose.

'I see the nose, but what now?' is probably the next thought on your mind. Okay, first things first, size matters when we are looking at the Marriage Palace.

Is it too big, or too small?

Now, at this point you might be thinking, wait a minute, size is relative. I might think it is small but someone else might think it is big. How will I know? The answer is to judge it in proportion to her face size. If a lady's face is wide, a slightly bigger nose will be considered 'average' size, whereas if her face is narrow, a small nose is considered 'average'.

Lady with small nose

Now, when it comes to the nose of a lady, we like it to be average sized. Why? Well, if her nose is too large, this is known in Face Reading as a 'Lonely Mountain Formation' (孤峰獨聳).

A 'Lonely Mountain Formation' is the term used to describe a face where all the other features are dwarfed by the nose. As a result, this person is lonely. What does lonely mean? It denotes an old age with no children around you and sometimes, a financially tight or difficult old age. Definitely not what we consider a 'good life' for a woman.

Much more important for a lady, when it comes to evaluating her nose, is the nose bridge. A good nose bridge is straight and charismatic, indicating a husband who is a capable and talented individual. An excellent nose is one with a straight charismatic nose bridge and a rounded nose tip with fleshy nostril wings – this indicates not just a capable and talented husband, but one who is wealthy as well!

Lady with fleshy nose

Sometimes, people don't want to know about their spouse, but rather, whether or not a spousal relationship is happy.

Now, in the study of Mian Xiang, the eyes, are not just the window to the soul, but the person's heart.

How do you know if someone is sad? You look at her eyes. How do you know if someone is happy? Well, you also look at her eyes! The eyes reveal the emotional state of the person. To tell if a person is happy or not happy with her relationship, all you have to do is look at her eyes.

So what then are you looking for?

Watery, dark, glossy eyes indicate a marriage or relationship in trouble. Sharp alert eyes indicate a fruitful and happy relationship. Yes, it really is that simple!

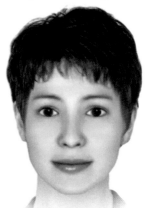

Eyes are sharp and clear

If people have eyes that are deep set (meaning, sunken into the face, or seem set deep back in the face – see picture below), these people are people who are constantly troubled emotionally. Their relationship or marriage is deeply unsatisfactory. If you see people with deep-set eyes and their eyes look tired and gloomy, you can be sure it is unhappiness that is not caused by too much action in the bedroom!

Eyes are gloomy and dull

Spot the Good Husband a Mile Away

面相

Well, not literally of course but with some of the knowledge you have garnered from this book, it is possible to spot a good husband (or a good wife – ladies first, so I will get to the wife spotting shortly).

Now, it is often the case that a person (male or female) is one thing during the courtship phase and quite another character altogether sometimes, when the ring is on the finger! Hence, I do get a lot of single ladies who ask me how they will know a prospective boyfriend will be a good husband!

It's always a tricky question to answer. I travel all over the world to teach Mian Xiang and I have to remember that in the US, the answer is quite different from what I would say in Malaysia! Different cultures have different standards on what makes a good spouse. Of course, whether or not a person will be a good husband depends on what you personally like.

However, I think it is quite safe to assume that generally, the standard of rich and wealthy AND faithful are the essential basics that every lady would like her husband to possess!

I always explain to my students (or audience members) that these are not the only criteria in looking for a good husband.

You must also consider if this person will make a good father, a trustworthy friend and a reliable person. What's the use of being rich if he is not reliable? And most importantly, you need to check if he's compatible with his wife! He may be the BEST person in the world but might not make a good husband to you because by nature, he is solitary and not an affectionate person.

I have compiled a basic check list but ladies, please, remember, these are not rules carved in stone but simple guidelines okay? You must remember that there are exceptions!

Okay, the first stop is his nose. You want to check that your man has a good nose. Why? Well, the nose is a man's Wealth Palace so if you want to marry a rich man, you've got to first start with someone who has great wealth capacity.

Now, what is a good nose? Check that the nose bridge is straight and broad, the nose tip is rounded and fleshy, the nostril wings are broad and most importantly, the nostrils are not visible when you look the person in the face from the front.

Nosebridge is straight and broad. Nose tip is rounded and fleshy.

A crooked nose with a pointy sharp tip denotes a cunning and dishonest man. Definitely not husband material!

Visible nostrils indicate a spendthrift – now, it doesn't matter how big his nose tip is or how fleshy his nose wings are, it's no point having plenty of wealth capacity if he fritters it all away!

Oh, and nose hair. Not only is it a real turn off, but ladies, this guy will barely have enough money to sustain himself let alone take care of you.

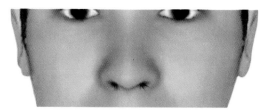

Exposed nasal hair

Check the nose bridge! Make sure the bridge is not low, as in the picture below. If his nose bridge is low, and he has downward growing eyebrow hair, his self-esteem is low. The last time I checked, most ladies weren't too keen on marrying doormat husbands. You want a confident man for a husband.

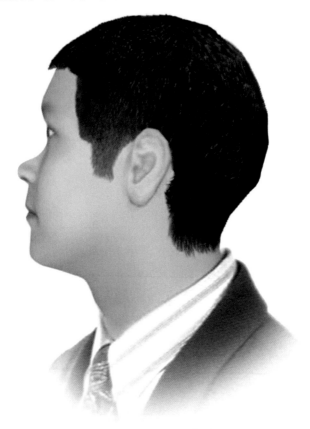

Low nose bridge

Bumps on his nose bridge are telling of a short temper, especially if his eyebrow hair grows upwards. Upward growing eyebrow hair not only makes a person look fierce, but when coupled with bumps on the nose bridge, indicates the person has a short fuse.

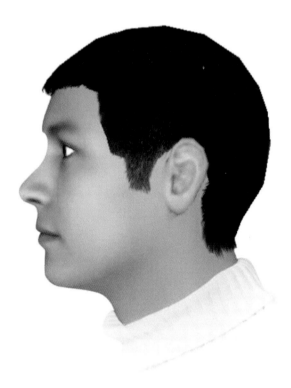

High nose bridge

You also want to check for lines across the nose – if your prospective husband has vertical lines across his nose, this indicates incompatibility with his spouse or a likelihood of the relationship going cold after some time. It is important to realise that this is not the fault of the spouse – it does not matter who this man is with, things will eventually go cold relationship-wise.

Now, we all tell a white lie once in a while but no one wants to marry a habitual liar. So beware of the guy with thin lips –

not only does he like talking a lot, but you might find amongst all that talk is a lot of fibbing! Especially if those thin lips are accompanied by a crooked nose!

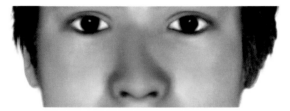

Crooked nose

So, assuming the nose is good, we move on next to the forehead. You want a man with a high and broad forehead, like the picture below.

High, broad and smooth (no dents) forehead.

A high and broad forehead indicates not only an ambitious individual but also someone who will rise up the ranks and gain social status. This is a man who is intelligent and possesses good analytical skills. Why are the analytical skills important? Well, you don't want to marry a guy who can't figure out how to solve your basic household issues or problems right? Or someone who is always wringing his hands without a clue what to do when faced with a difficulty?

It is important not to confuse high and broad, with foreheads that are high but bulging, especially in the center, like in the picture below.

Bulging foreheads, especially those that bulge in the middle, belong to lonely people. Uneven bumps on a high forehead indicate poor analytical and thinking abilities.

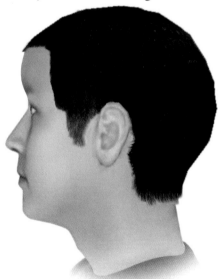

Slightly bulging forehead.

A recent addition to the checklist was the sentimental husband. By sentimental, I don't mean he likes mushy music or enjoys going to see chick flicks. When I say sentimental, I mean he is a gentle kind-hearted person, who values the importance of building and maintaining good relationships.

To tell how gentle the person is, look at his eyes. You want a guy with slightly bigger eyes, as this signifies a person who is emotionally kind and has a good heart. Gentle looking eyes belong to kind hearted people. Piercing eyes with a sharp glare belong to those who are ruthless. So remember, don't just look at his nose – look into his eyes too!

Gentle eyes   *Fierce eyes*

Now, of course you won't find so many perfect features in any one guy, so you have to prioritise your requirements. Sometimes you might find a guy who will be wealthy and rich, but has an extremely short temper. Or he might be sweet and sentimental, but not QUITE as wealthy as you would like him to be.

I have heard the common statement, 'Oh he'll change, I just know it'. Or perhaps you think you can whip him into shape once you've married him.

There is a saying in Chinese – Age 3 Determines 80 三歲定八十, which means, your basic nature at age 3 will remain until you are 80! A person's basic nature will not change much. Even in face reading, which is to a certain degree dynamic, a person's face can change over the years but their bone structure does not change much. It might be more meaty or less meaty, a bump or scar or two may appear over the years, but that's basically it.

So don't expect to change a person's character drastically. This might be an uphill battle with not much to show for at the end.

You might also want to look for 'potential' and look at long term aspects of a person. Don't just look at short term and the now. A person may not be rich 'now' but this does not mean he won't be in future. Likewise, a seemingly promising guy might not be as good in the long run.

Ultimately, basic character sometimes is a lot more important than things like wealth, so ladies, think carefully about what those ideal features in your man should be!

Wanted: A Good Woman

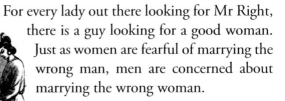

For every lady out there looking for Mr Right, there is a guy looking for a good woman. Just as women are fearful of marrying the wrong man, men are concerned about marrying the wrong woman.

Gone are the days where a man could have a wife, a few concubines at home and everybody lived as one big happy family. In the old days, even up to the end of Qing Dynasty (1911) and the early Republic era of China, a man was regarded as successful only if he had at least 3 main wives and four concubines. Today, marrying the wrong woman is not just an emotionally draining situation, but can be expensive. Just ask Donald Trump how expensive!

Even in this era of the pre-nuptial agreement, marrying the wrong woman still entails a lot of emotional hassle.

Most guys I know would be quite happy to find a nice, loving, gentle, amicable, intelligent lady who will be the perfect wife and caring mother to his children. The epitome of the Chinese saying, can go into the kitchen, can come out to the living room! (出得廳堂，入得廚房).

Now guys, you have the perfect excuse to look deep into her eyes because her eyes are the first thing you should evaluate. A woman's eyes reveal her emotional state. Big eyeballs that are watery or glossy are often attractive because they indicate the lady in question has Peach Blossom appeal but they also indicate a person who can be overly emotional.

A quick note on Peach Blossom. Peach Blossoms are a type of flower culturally associated with romance in China and Chinese culture. When the Chinese say you are enjoying 'peach blossom luck' they are essentially saying you are enjoying good 'romance' luck.

If you can handle the histrionics that sometimes accompany overly-emotional ladies, that's okay but if you prefer a more stable emotional state, those big eyes are really not a feature you want to have in your prospective wife.

Droopy or eyes that slant downwards, as in the picture below, belong to overly-possessive ladies who are often very suspicious and clingy. You know, the kind that has your mobile number on speed-dial and who wants to know where you are every half an hour. If you love the attention, then fine.

But if not, avoid ladies with this feature!

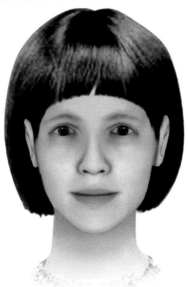

Droopy eyes that slant downwards

Next, you must look at her nose. You do want to choose a woman that 'brings luck' to her man right? This is how you do it. Check her nose. A bit of reverse logic is required to understand the significance of this feature. The nose is the lady's Husband Star Bi Wei Fu Xing 鼻爲夫星. So, looking at her nose is a bit like looking at yourself – if she's got a good nose, it means you, her husband, are also good.

What are the key good features when it comes to reading the nose of a lady? If her nose bridge is low and her nose tip is thin, her husband would not be someone who is capable or wealthy. You don't really want to be this guy!

Her nose bridge should not be overly high – a very high nose bridge indicates a lady with a very strong, even overly strong, opinion. Unless you enjoy a dominating character as your wife, you might prefer to find a lady friend (or wife) with a not-to-high nose bridge.

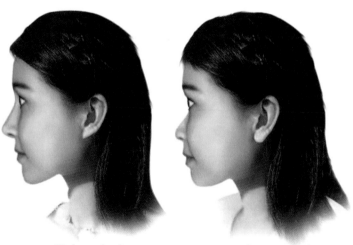

High nosebridge   *Low nosebridge*

You want her to have a nice rounded nose tip, fleshy nostrils and of course, nostrils that are not visible when seen from the front. All these are indicators of a good husband star, a husband who is successful and wealthy.

Fleshy cheeks supporting a fleshy nose

Guys usually want to know – is my wife going to be supportive of my career? Is she going to be able to help me in my work? The answer to this lies on her cheeks.

Her cheeks should be fleshy. If the cheeks are fleshy, they are supporting the good nose, indicating a wife who is not just supportive, but helpful to her husband. In Chinese, we call these combined features "Prospering the Husband" Wang Fu 旺夫 meaning – the man gains good fortune after marriage to the woman.

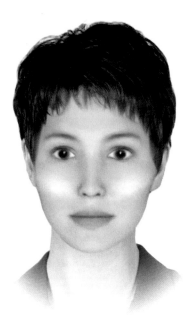

Large bony cheek with small nose

What you don't want are bony cheeks. Yes, be certain that the cheeks are actually supportive, not bony. Large bony cheeks belong to women who far from bringing good fortune to their husbands, actually suppress their husbands because their husbands are incapable or ineffective. Large bony cheeks on a lady usually indicate an unsuccessful marriage.

Why? Because bony cheeks will suppress the nose. Remember, the nose is the husband star for a woman – if her cheek bones are 'squeezing' the nose, that is literally the situation in the marriage. In Chinese, this is called 女奪夫權 Nu Duo Fu Quan (Female Stealing the Power from the Husband).

The forehead of a lady is also an important consideration when choosing a good wife. I know this is the age of the working wife but this is of course not always ideal in a marriage situation (although I know there are men who do not mind this).

Generally, a broad square forehead indicates career ladies who have strong unyielding characters. They are often active decision makers as well so may not make for good housewife (or mother) material if you cannot handle this. If a docile housewife is what you are looking for, then look for a lady with a gently rounded forehead. What do I mean by round or square? To discern this, look at the hairline on the forehead. If the hairline runs across the forehead in a straight line, then the lady in question has a square forehead. If the hairline curves gently down the side of the temples, then the lady in question has a rounded forehead. It's that simple.

Rounded forehead

Squarish forehead

Do remember that the forehead of the lady must match her chin. A round fleshy chin may not be supermodel material or the stuff of trophy wives, but it denotes a good old age, surrounded by filial children and grandchildren. If your wife has a great old age, this denotes you, her husband, are successful because you are able to give her this good life. Also, in Chinese culture, a man is considered to have a good old age if he has 'a house full of sons and grandchildren' (子孫滿堂 Zi Sun Man Tang) – so if your wife has a good old age, don't you think you'll be in the same wonderful picture?

One, Two or a Football Team?
Checking for child-bearing abilities

In many consultations for Feng Shui and BaZi (Destiny Analysis), the question of fertility increasingly pops up. It seems as society gets more fast-paced, having children is not as easy as it seems! It is a great concern to many women (and men) that their partners be fertile.

It's of course not something that people can openly discuss. Unlike bank statements or net worth, all which can be easily checked upon, you can't inquire about this without an invasive procedure, try before you buy as it were, or suggest a hire-lease agreement. Marriage is for many a once in a lifetime event.

Good news! Embarrassing questions or medical procedures are not required to find out if your prospective spouse (male and female!) is fertile. All you have to do is observe the philtrum.

In Mian Xiang studies, the philtrum is the only part of the face that should be sunken and broad. The philtrum tells you if, pardon my language, the plumbing for your spouse, male or female, is working properly.

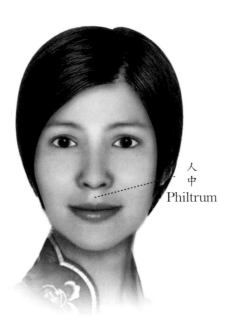

人中
Philtrum

For the lady, the philtrum represents her uterus – if this feature is short in length or narrow and tight, this suggests difficulty in conceiving or difficulties giving birth.

For the man, the philtrum also represents 'his tool' but you have to judge one more feature, that is the mouth in tandem with the philtrum to ascertain a man's fertility. If a man's philtrum is tight and he has a small mouth, this may suggest a low sperm count.

If the philtrum is tight and short, the mouth is small AND the chin is sharp, these are definitive indicators of low reproductive capabilities. Let me explain why – you see, Face Reading, like all Chinese Metaphysical sciences, utilises and is based on the Five Elements theory. The Mouth represents Water, which in the study of the Five Elements, relates to reproductive capabilities, specifically, a man's sperm.

A small mouth denotes weak Water, whilst a sharp chin denotes loneliness in old age. In Chinese culture, loneliness in old age means 'no children'.

Now, Face Reading is not just about the features in isolation, but the whole picture – a tight philtrum, small mouth, sharp chin all add up to no pitter patter of little feet. Hence, poor reproductive capabilities in such a person.

What does a Flirt look like?

Next to relationships, the one thing many women want to know is how they can tell if their spouse will be faithful. Now, I must urge some caution when reading this section. As a responsible ethical teacher, it is my job to ensure that my readers appreciate this key point: do not be paranoid if you find any of these features on your spouse's face. Remember, features only indicate potential – these features do not have to manifest themselves. A person cannot use his or her facial features as an excuse for his or her behavior.

Also, features that suggest a person is a flirt do not necessarily mean this person will engage in extra-marital affairs. A man who has more female friends or close female friends is not always unfaithful so keep a rein on the suspicion level okay?

On then to the 'flirt features'.

Have you noticed how certain stars in showbiz, often the ladies men, have crinkles or crow's feet on the sides of their eyes when they smile?

Long fish tails

These are called Fish Tails (魚尾蚊) in face reading and are the lines that are visible by the side of a man's eyes when he smiles. Fish Tails denote a smooth and often flirtatious character who likes to mingle with the ladies. These gentlemen are also usually very successful if they are in a business that requires selling to the opposite sex!

Now, its one thing to like mingling with the ladies, but quite another thing to turn a casual friendship into a dalliance. Whether or not a man will engage in extra-marital affairs depends on whether or not the Fish Tails pierce the Spouse Palace.

Remember, the man's Spouse Palace is not the nose, but located just at the temples. If the Fish Tails do not touch or pierce the Spouse Palace, then your man is just a flirt – he looks, he chats but he does not touch!

What you need to be worried about are Peach Blossom eyes coupled with Fish Tails. These are the lady killers. What are Peach Blossom eyes? They are what are termed as 'bedroom eyes' – big, glossy, almost wet looking eyes, with long eye lashes and curved elegant eyebrows.

These eyes attract opposite sex like a moth to a flame and if your spouse or boyfriend has this feature, well, this might be the reason for your attraction in the first place!

Now, men with Peach Blossom eyes may have every intention of being faithful to their spouses. They may even not want the extra attention. But they just can't seem to escape attention.

The lips are another feature to be evaluated. An overly plump or fleshy lower lip, as in the picture below, indicates a person who is excited by being with someone other than their spouse or has a very strong sex drive. A person with an over-developed lower lip (both male and female) needs to be constantly satisfied physically or they will be prone to looking for fulfillment elsewhere. If you find that your spouse has this feature, you need to take matters into your own hands!

Thick lower lips

The Rich Person's Face

The question on 'Will I Be Rich?' is almost a must in Astrology or BaZi consults. Now, if you are reading faces – what do you look for?

There are two important things to bear in mind: wealth capacity and wealth luck. You need to differentiate between the two when evaluating a person's wealth via their face.

Wealth capacity focuses on the person's ability to amass wealth during his or her lifetime. Wealth luck is of course focusing on the present career or wealth outlook. So, decide what you want to find out. It goes without saying of course that capacity is a lot more important than luck, since luck can change and improve.

To check a person's wealth capacity, begin with the nose. The nose represents the Wealth Palace for both sexes. A nice, rounded, fleshy tip coupled with fleshy, wide, unexposed nostrils indicates a good Wealth Palace. Of course, the quality of the nose is determined by the cheeks, clarity of the person's forehead and Life Palace.

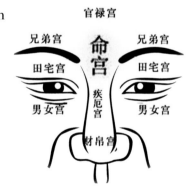

The nose must be supported and the cheeks are the Left and Right Hand Ministers to the Emperor (the nose). If the person's cheeks are low setting, then even if the nose looks charismatic, the person will not be wealthy. Merely having a big nose does not forbode good fortune in terms of wealth capacity. You must match the nose with the cheeks.

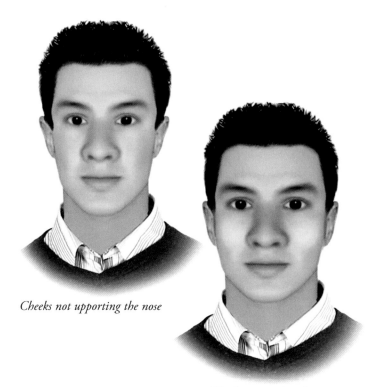

Cheeks not supporting the nose

Cheeks supporting the nose

This is because cheeks represent a person's authority and power. With great wealth comes great power. Cheeks represent leadership. Think about it – for people to become wealthy, they must be leaders in their own right. If they cannot lead, chances are they are not that wealthy.

What about the forehead then – why do we need to look at the quality of the forehead? Because the forehead represents a person's career and social status. For a person to be wealthy, he or she has obviously got to have a fabulous career and great social status. Thus a high, broad and fleshy forehead is essential to becoming a wealthy person.

High, broad and fleshy forehead

What about the bedroom millionaire? Of course, there are the rare few that make money in their pajamas, people earning their living through options trading for example. Successful people in these fields are rare but not non-existent. However, their faces would have slightly different key aspects. Instead of supporting cheeks, they would have a more dominant forehead and supporting ears. This is because becoming wealthy without the need to influence others often denotes a more lonely but highly intelligent character. Taller and broader foreheads coupled with long, fleshy ears fit these personality characteristics. People in this field will also have slightly narrower chins due to the solitary nature of their work.

Finding a Good Teacher

Once a concerned mother came to me and said she wanted to hire a private tutor for her son. She wanted to know if there was any way to tell if the person was a good teacher! I thought this was a unique question but also, in light of the importance of a good education these days for youngsters, a very valid question.

She told me something I believe is very true - that mere 'qualifications' or credentials are not a good enough indication if someone is a 'good teacher'.

A good teacher is someone who must obviously know what they are teaching and more importantly, can teach the material without confusing the child. So, you do not want a confused person with messy thinking as your child's tutor.

Therefore, look carefully at the eyebrows of the prospective tutor or tuition teacher – they should not be messy, meaning, the eyebrow hair grows in different directions.

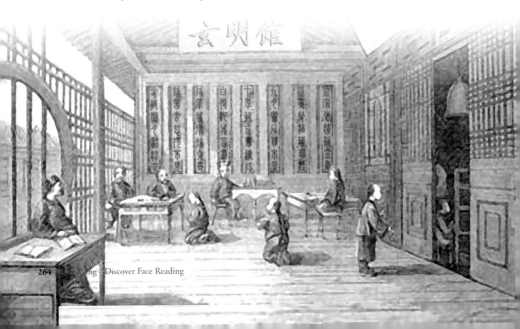

Face shapes are also helpful in selecting a suitable tutor for your child. In the study of the Five Elements. Wood represents education and progressive learning. A Wood element face denotes someone who is patient and effective, a person who is learned and philosophical.

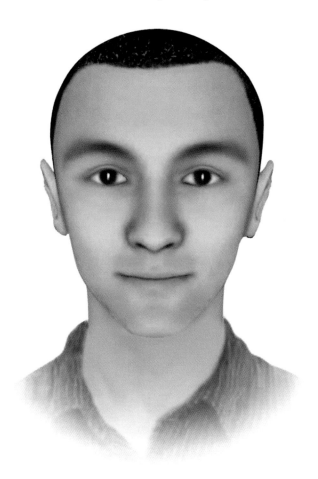

Wood element faces make good teachers

A good teacher also has to be patient – so avoid individuals with puffy faces or puffy cheeks like the picture below. This denotes a person who is hasty and temperamental, and who will be impatient with your child.

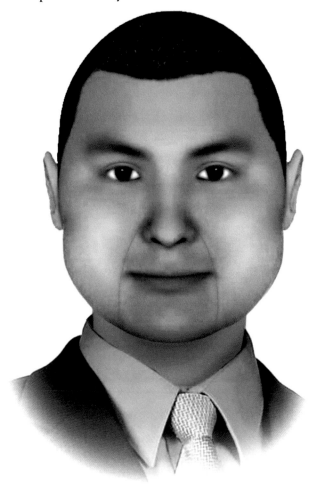

Puffy face

Faces to Avoid:
Cunning and Ungrateful People

One of the best reasons for most people learning face reading is to be able, at a glance, to determine if a person is trustworthy or whether a person has ill-intentions.

I thought I would include here a few tips on knowing how to identify these characteristics through a person's face. However, remember that it takes two or more features to be present in a face in order to determine if the person's intentions are good or bad. More importantly, the gestures or subtle movements of the person need to be considered at the time he or she is speaking to you in order to ascertain if it was sincere or dishonest speech that you heard.

Triangular Eyes

A person's eyes tell you a lot about the person's nature. Is he or she a good person? Is he or she harbouring ill-intentions? It's all in the eyes. One of the easiest ways to judge a person's sincerity and heart is to look at the shape of his or her eyes. Triangular eyes are sometimes described as 'hooded' eyes or eyes that look triangular in shape.

Triangular eyes, like in the picture below, often belong to those who constantly seek to 'get the better' of somebody else. Their innate nature is to always look to have the upper hand or better deal. They will not want to 'lose out' in a game or business. People with triangular eyes normally want to take advantage of others.

Triangular eyes

Also, take note of his or her gaze as he or she speaks to you. Eye contact will give you a level of understanding regarding his or her sincerity.

Exposed Jaw Bone

Of course, no one likes an ingrate and while no one will say that they do favours in the hope of being repaid, we certainly don't want to do things for ungrateful people either.

An exposed jawbone, meaning, the person's jaw is very strong and is one of the most dominant features on the face, tells us a person is the ungrateful type. What do I mean by ungrateful? This means that the person is cold in his or her conduct, especially in business. He or she does not consider good deeds done for him or her to be something to be grateful or thankful for.

Exposed jaw bone

Sometimes, it is not because he or she is rude or wicked – instead, he or she simply forgets what you have done for him or her or will not remember how you have helped him or her in the past. These are people who, if you should decide to help them, you should do it without expecting anything in return. Otherwise, you're only asking for disappointment.

A Crook's Nose

The crooked nose belongs to a person who does not have good or pure intentions, especially when money is involved. Crooked noses indeed belong to crooks.

Now, do not be confused with a 'bent' nose. When I say a nose is crooked, I mean it is bumpy, boney and the bridge is not straight. The nose looks twisted and edgy. If the nose tip is also sharp, this person is just not to be trusted. He or she is as cunning as a fox!

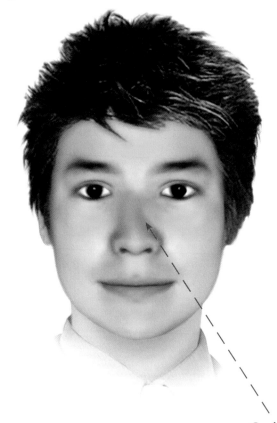

Crooked nose

Thin Lips Speak Lies

Always be wary of people with thin lips – I certainly am. People with thin lips usually talk a lot and it is not just talk, but often sweet talk. The ones to really watch out for are those with thin lips and who have triangular eyes, especially if you are planning to buy something from them. These people are most likely not telling the truth when they speak to you and would not hesitate to lie to get what they want.

Thin lips

The Loyal And Filial Look

Now, how do you know if a person will be loyal as a friend or employee? How do you determine if a person is filial? Firstly, look for long eyebrows (long meaning at least eye length) that are not excessively bushy. Eyebrows represent the Siblings Palace. Where the eyebrows are complete, meaning they are long and unbroken, it denotes the person values brotherhood (or sisterhood) amongst friends, is altruistic and places great importance on relationships. Such people will not betray a friend's trust in them.

You also want a person with a straight nose since this indicates an honest person and a fleshy chin. Finally, check to make sure they have ears that are flat against the side of the ears (not sticking out like Dumbo) and the borders of their ears are clearly defined.

貼
面
耳 *Ears that are flat against the side of the ears*

The Intelligent and Wise Person

Why is this category significant? Well, every organization needs a wise advisor or perhaps a smart thinker who will solve problems. This is the kind of person you want in operations, helping you solve problems and not just whine about them.

Remember that intelligent does not mean a person who scores in exams. That is not intelligence, but scholastic / academic luck or ability. An intelligent person does not always have a good report card! An intelligent and wise person is one who can think, analyse, solve problems and make use of his or her knowledge well. It's not what you know but what you do with what you know that counts.

So what are you looking for in a person who is going to help you strategies or come up with good solutions to problems? Well, you want high set ears, meaning, the tips of the ears are level with or higher than the eyebrow. One of the key indicators of intelligence is the height of the ears. Ears that are the same level or higher than the eyebrow indicate intelligence. Obviously, the higher the ears are set, the greater the intelligence.

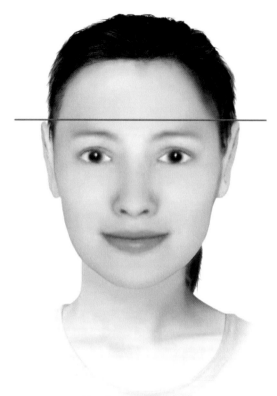

Ears higher than eyebrows

We are talking about height, not size here. We are concerned with the level the ears are set at, not their size.

Second feature that must compliment high setting ears is the forehead. Without a doubt, a high forehead denotes better analytical and thinking power as opposed to a low forehead. Now, a word of caution: bumpy foreheads that are high are not considered intelligent. Remember – we are looking for broad, fleshy, smooth and high foreheads. Bumpy high foreheads are considered bad foreheads, belonging to people who have poor analytical and thinking power. Bumpy foreheads denote distorted thinking!

The eyes represent the clarity of one's heart and mind. Dull, weak looking or glazed looking eyes do not indicate clarity of mind. Conversely, sharp, alert and radiant eyes belong to those who are smart, wise and intelligent.

Eyes are clear and sharp

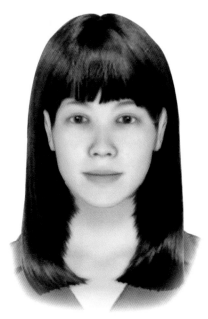

Eyes are droopy and gloomy

These features, coupled together, indicate a person who can think through problems and issues, who is solution orientated and who will dispense wise advice, not empty eggs.

Spotting The Scrooge

When I give talks at corporations on face reading, often, people are keen to know how to identify a scrooge, or to put it more diplomatically, a thrifty person. This is especially useful for those who are in sales.

People who are thrifty tend to have smaller nostrils, as in the picture below.

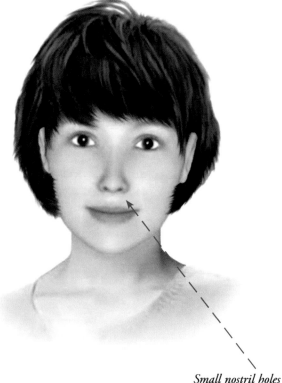

Small nostril holes

People with bigger nostrils spend money faster than others. This is because the nose is the Wealth Palace. If you have big nostrils, the Wealth Qi leaks out much more easily!

People with sharp pointy noses tend to be calculative, especially if they also have a puffy Property Palace. Why? A sharp nose indicates the tendency to measure 'value' a lot. These people are shrewd when it comes to money. A puffy Property Palace often denotes the need to feel 'abundant', so the need to 'have more'. Their attitude is somewhat greedy. Put the two together and you have a miserly self-centered person.

Here's a secret to dealing with these types of customers – don't walk away, but always make them feel like they're getting a bargain. This way, they will respond to your sales pitch better.

Mean People

When I say mean, I am not talking about just a person who is not nice. I mean people who talk about you behind your back, bad mouth you and start rumours about other people. They are not people you want in your life, or even near you!

How then do you make sure you avoid such people? First, keep away from people who have faces with tight looking skin. Tight looking skin on the face makes the person look like his or her face is pulled tightly back. The nose will usually be flat and the nostrils are clearly visible.

People with tight looking faces are prone to jealousy and will not hesitate to talk bad about you the moment you turn your back.

If someone you know has eyes and mouth that are very close to their nose, this is someone you don't want to get to know too well. They will not hesitate to tell you exactly what they think if they don't like something.

Puffy faced individuals who also have triangular eyes are the jealous types. Normally, people who are jealous tend to be vengeful when they don't get what they want. So it is always good to know the people who are likely to turn into green-eyed monsters.

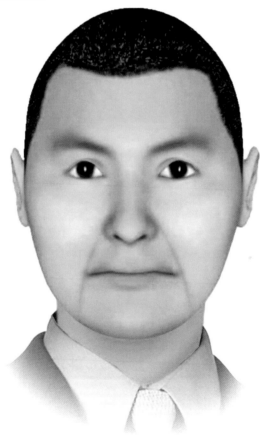

Puffy face and triangular eyes

Face Reading: Art and Judgment

面相

Perhaps by now, you might be feeling a little bit intimidated. Don't be. Face reading requires some practice and sometimes, you have to 'see' the features in a person before you can recognize them. Also, face reading is an art – there are subtleties and nuances that will only become visible with practice. So keep practicing and the appreciation of a person's face will come.

Since you are learning these techniques through reading and not in a live class, sometimes, it takes a little more time (and perhaps a little bit of imagination of the descriptions in this book)!

In time, you will realise that truly, we are all unique. Yes, every person has a pair of eyes, ears, eyebrows, nose and mouth, but the variations in those features are almost infinite. You will read everyone's face instinctively.

Once you are familiar with the features and contours of the face, you know how to read a good face and a bad face. You will see that in fact, it's very simple to tell if a person is enjoying good fortune or going through bad luck.

A beaming, radiant face with a genuine smile tells you that a person is enjoying good fortune. Sounds so simplistic and straightforward? You know what? Nobody said Face Reading is not about common sense nor did anyone say it has to be difficult! So trust in those instincts. In face reading, your initial judgment or 'feel' of the face is an important instinctive evaluation you must not discount.

Good fortune faces are usually 'happy' faces. Of course you might say 'yeah but some people can pretend to be happy'. True. That is why you need to learn to be a judge of 'genuine' happy faces. When a person smiles – check to see if the eyes are smiling! And check if the 'cheeks' were forced to smile. A forced smile is a faked 'happiness'. Take a good hard look the next time at a smiling person who you know is facing a difficult situation – his eyes are not smiling even if his mouth is. It's that simple.

People facing bad luck will look gloomy, teary eyed and will seem as if a dark cloud is hovering over their head. Now I am not talking about the tired look after you come back from a hard day's work. I am talking about when you first observe the person – early in the day. If at first glance, you get a sense of the person being gloomy, his luck for that period in his life cannot be that good!

In the old days, all formal face readings was done only during daylight hours. While some of the techniques in this book can be applied at any time, it is important, especially at the beginner's stage, that you engage in face reading in a place with sufficient brightness or lighting so you could see each feature clearly.

What About Cosmetic Surgery?
Can I 'fix' my face?

The first thing I get asked in any seminar on face reading is: will a plastic surgeon fix my problems? Cosmetic surgery might not 'change' your fortune substantially; however it does change how you 'feel' about yourself. And sometimes, this can help.

You see, if you feel 'good' about yourself, you change your 'heart'. And we all know, if you change your heart, your face will reflect that change. Your fortunes change subsequently.

It is arguable if cosmetic surgery can change that much of your destiny as it is difficult to change some things. Can you change your eyeballs? The location of your ears? The bone structure of your forehead or jaw, the height and size of your eyes? You might also want to ask yourself if recent well-known celebrities who have gone under the knife have in fact experienced a positive change in fortunes.

The simple removal of scars and lines can of course create a significant effect. I've asked many clients who have certain negative lines, like a line piercing through the Life Palace, to have these lines 'botoxed' or removed.

When these lines were removed, my clients reported significant improvement in their daily lives. So I don't discount the power of modern science and cosmetic surgery but, I must say, it is not the answer for every instance and certainly not something to be actively encouraged.

A Personal Perspective on Face Reading

From my 2005 Face Reading Seminar

Many people ask me this question. They ask me – Joey, do you always chose your friends according to their faces?

It surprises them when I say 'No'. The next question that pops up is always "But why? You can read their faces!"

Yes, but that doesn't mean I pass judgment on every single person who wants to be my friend. I'm not perfect and so I can't expect people around me to be that way.

I have friends who have features that indicate they are cunning and jealous when it comes to money matters. So? That just means I don't do business with them. I don't talk to them about money – we can be buddies and hang out together. Our friendship is okay.

I know friends who have low self-esteem – a low nose bridge, downward growing, sparse eyebrows. These people are still my friends. I still share my happiness, disappointments, success and friendship with them.

Of course I also meet people who are compulsive liars. With these people, I keep my distance and have nothing more than a casual friendship. I take everything they say with a pinch of salt.

Your spouse will not be perfect. There will be features that might not be too ideal that you've probably discovered by now. If you find these features in your spouse, the first thing is to acknowledge these setbacks and recognize these are part of the person. They may not be changeable. It's a different story if you find less favourable features on your own face.

You can make a conscious decision to change them. How you might ask? Well to change your face, change the heart! Remember in chapter One I said '相由心生 Xiang You Xin Sheng'? Your face features comes from your heart. If you change your attitude, behaviour and thoughts, your features will eventually reflect that. And this is a change that no plastic surgeon's blade can achieve.

Beyond the Surface

I hope this book has given you a good introduction to the fascinating subject of Chinese Face Reading and I hope that you have fun practicing what you have learnt and I am sure you will find it a useful and handy skill to have on hand. Certainly, no face will ever be the same again after you have read this book, trust me!

Many of the techniques I have shown you here are merely simple introductory techniques for Face Reading – there is more than one way to skin a cat and more than one way to read certain attributes or characteristics from a face. The idea is to keep things simple and easy in this book, but by no means is what I have discussed in this book an exhaustive list of the applications and techniques in Face Reading.

In my next book, I will share with you more techniques and 'secrets' of the Chinese Art of Face Reading, including how to undertake Multiple Position Readings and insights into the Five Officers in face reading, the Eyes, Nose, Ear, Mouth and Brows. I will share with you techniques to judging a person not just from the fixed facial features, but from small gestures such as blinking and even, how to evaluate pimples on your face!

In the meantime, happy face reading!

About Joey Yap

Joey Yap is the founder of the Mastery Academy of Chinese Metaphysics, a global organization devoted to the teaching of Feng Shui, BaZi, Mian Xiang and other Chinese Metaphysics subjects. He is also the Chief Consultant of Joey Yap Consulting Group, an international consulting firm specialising in Feng Shui and Chinese Astrology services and audits.

Joey Yap is the bestselling author of over 60 books on Feng Shui, Chinese Astrology, Face Reading and Yi Jing, many of which have topped the Malaysian and Singaporean MPH bookstores' bestseller lists.

Thousands of students from all around the world have learnt and mastered Classical Feng Shui, Chinese Astrology, and other Chinese Metaphysics subjects through Joey Yap's structured learning programs, books and online training. Joey Yap's courses are currently taught by over 30 instructors worldwide.

Every year Joey Yap conducts his 'Feng Shui and Astrology' seminar to a crowd of more than 3500 people at the Kuala Lumpur Convention Center. He also takes this annual seminar on a world tour to Frankfurt, San Francisco, New York, Toronto, London, Sydney and Singapore.

In addition to being a regular guest on various radio and TV shows, Joey Yap has also written columns for The New Straits Times and The Star - Malaysia's two leading newspapers. He has also been featured in many popular global publications and networks like Time International, Forbes International, the International Herald Tribune and Bloomberg.

He has also hosted his own TV series, 'Discover Feng Shui with Joey Yap', on 8TV, a local Malaysian network in 2005; and 'Walking The Dragons with Joey Yap' on Astro Wah Lai Toi, Malaysia's cable network in 2008.

Joey Yap has worked with HSBC, Bloomberg, Microsoft, Samsung, IBM, HP, Alliance, Great Eastern, Citibank, Standard Chartered, OCBC, SIME UEP, Mah Sing, Auto Bavaria, Volvo, AXA, Singtel, ABN Amro, CIMB, Hong-Leong, Manulife and others.

Author's personal website :**www.joeyyap.com**

Joey Yap on Facebook:

 www.facebook.com/JoeyYapFB

EDUCATION

The Mastery Academy of Chinese Metaphysics:
the first choice for practitioners and aspiring students of the art and science of Chinese Classical Feng Shui and Astrology.

For thousands of years, Eastern knowledge has been passed from one generation to another through the system of discipleship. A venerated master would accept suitable individuals at a young age as his disciples, and informally through the years, pass on his knowledge and skills to them. His disciples in turn, would take on their own disciples, as a means to perpetuate knowledge or skills.

This system served the purpose of restricting the transfer of knowledge to only worthy honourable individuals and ensuring that outsiders or Westerners would not have access to thousands of years of Eastern knowledge, learning and research.

However, the disciple system has also resulted in Chinese Metaphysics and Classical Studies lacking systematic teaching methods. Knowledge garnered over the years has not been accumulated in a concise, systematic manner, but scattered amongst practitioners, each practicing his/her knowledge, art and science, in isolation.

The disciple system, out of place in today's modern world, endangers the advancement of these classical fields that continue to have great relevance and application today.

At the Mastery Academy of Chinese Metaphysics, our Mission is to bring Eastern Classical knowledge in the fields of metaphysics, Feng Shui and Astrology sciences and the arts to the world. These Classical teachings and knowledge, previously shrouded in secrecy and passed on only through the discipleship system, are adapted into structured learning, which can easily be understood, learnt and mastered. Through modern learning methods, these renowned ancient arts, sciences and practices can be perpetuated while facilitating more extensive application and understanding of these classical subjects.

The Mastery Academy espouses an educational philosophy that draws from the best of the East and West. It is the world's premier educational institution for the study of Chinese Metaphysics Studies offering a wide range and variety of courses, ensuring that students have the opportunity to pursue their preferred field of study and enabling existing practitioners and professionals to gain cross-disciplinary knowledge that complements their current field of practice.

Courses at the Mastery Academy have been carefully designed to ensure a comprehensive yet compact syllabus. The modular nature of the courses enables students to immediately begin to put their knowledge into practice while pursuing continued study of their field and complementary fields. Students thus have the benefit of developing and gaining practical experience in tandem with the expansion and advancement of their theoretical knowledge.

Students can also choose from a variety of study options, from a distance learning program, the Homestudy Series, that enables study at one's own pace or intensive foundation courses and compact lecture-based courses, held in various cities around the world by Joey Yap or our licensed instructors. The Mastery Academy's faculty and make-up is international in nature, thus ensuring that prospective students can attend courses at destinations nearest to their country of origin or with a licensed Mastery Academy instructor in their home country.

The Mastery Academy provides 24x7 support to students through its Online Community, with a variety of tools, documents, forums and e-learning materials to help students stay at the forefront of research in their fields and gain invaluable assistance from peers and mentoring from their instructors.

MASTERY ACADEMY
OF CHINESE METAPHYSICS

www.masteryacademy.com

MALAYSIA
19-3, The Boulevard
Mid Valley City
59200 Kuala Lumpur, Malaysia
Tel : +603-2284 8080
Fax : +603-2284 1218
Email : info@masteryacademy.com

Australia, Austria, Canada, China, Croatia, Cyprus, Czech Republic, Denmark, France, Germany, Greece, Hungary, India, Italy, Kazakhstan, Malaysia, Netherlands (Holland), New Zealand, Philippines, Poland, Russian Federation, Singapore, Slovenia, South Africa, Switzerland, Turkey, U.S.A., Ukraine, United Kingdom

JOEY YAP'S
BAZI PROFILING SYSTEM

Unleashing personal potential to achieve peak performanc

The Path of Least Resistance to Success

Joey Yap's BaZi Profiling System is designed to help you make the most out of y protential and other people that matter to you. Using the proven BaZi (Chinese Astrolo system, Joey has simplified the process to analyze your character based on your Date and T of Birth, at three different levels. These levels function collectively as a means of provid categorical descriptions of your inborn personality traits, temperaments, behavioral patte suitable roles in life and your Path of Least Resistance to Success!

The fast and easy way to reveal the insights to your personality and career!

- Identify your areas of strength and possible areas of weakness in career and life

- Understand your own preference for personal development , career choices and organization effectiveness

- Capitalise on your natural tendency and strengths and use them to aid your career and your Pat to Success.

- View problems and challenges that come up at work as potential opportunities for greater succe

- Transform your business to achieve peak business performance by developing leaders and effect organization

www.baziprofiling.com

Introducing...
The Mastery Academy's E-Learning Center!

The Mastery Academy's goal has always been to share authentic knowledge of Chinese Metaphysics with the whole world.

Nevertheless, we do recognize that distance, time, and hotel and traveling costs – amongst many other factors – could actually hinder people from enrolling for a classroom-based course. But with the advent and amazing advance of IT today, NOT any more!

With this in mind, we have invested heavily in IT, to conceive what is probably the first and only E-Learning Center in the world today that offers a full range of studies in the field of Chinese Metaphysics.

Convenient   Study from Your   Easy Enrollment
                     Own Home

The Mastery Academy's E-Learning Center

Now, armed with your trusty computer or laptop, and Internet access, knowledge of classical Feng Shui, BaZi (Destiny Analysis) and Mian Xiang (Face Reading) are but a literal click away!

Study at your own pace, and interact with your Instructor and fellow students worldwide, from anywhere in the world. With our E-Learning Center, knowledge of Chinese Metaphysics is brought DIRECTLY to you in all its clarity – topic-by-topic, and lesson-by-lesson; with illustrated presentations and comprehensive notes expediting your learning curve!

Your education journey through our E-Learning Center may be done via any of the following approaches:

1. Online Courses

There are 3 Programs available: our Online Feng Shui Program, Online BaZi Program, and Online Mian Xiang Program. Each Program consists of several Levels, with each Level consisting of many Lessons in turn. Each Lesson contains a pre-recorded video session on the topic at hand, accompanied by presentation-slides and graphics as well as downloadable tutorial notes that you can print and file for future reference.

Video Lecture

Presentation
Slide

Downloadable
Notes

2. MA Live!

MA Live!, as its name implies, enables LIVE broadcasts of Joey Yap's courses and seminars – right to your computer screen. Students will not only get to see and hear Joey talk on real-time 'live', but also participate and more importantly, TALK to Joey via the MA Live! interface. All the benefits of a live class, minus the hassle of actually having to attend one!

How It Works

1.

2.

Our Live Classes   You at Home

3. Video-On-Demand (VOD)

Get immediate streaming-downloads of the Mastery Academy's wide range of educational DVDs, right on your computer screen. No more shipping costs and waiting time to be incurred!

**Instant VOD
Online**

1.

2.

Choose From Our list   Click "Play" on Your PC
of Available VODs!

Welcome to **www.maelearning.com**; the web portal of our E-Learning Center, and YOUR virtual gateway to Chinese Metaphysics!

Mastery Academy around the world

Canada

United States

United Kingdom

Denmark
Czech Republic
Austria
Switzerland
Poland
Netherlands
Germany
France Italy Solvenia
Cyprus Hungary
Greece Croatia

Russian
Federation

Ukraine

Turkey

Kazakhstan

India

China

Philippines

Kuala Lumpur
Malaysia

Singapore

Australia

South Africa

New Zealand

JOEY YAP CONSULTING GROUP

Joey Yap & Joey Yap Consulting Group

Headed by Joey Yap, Joey Yap Consulting Group (JYCG) is a leading international consulting firm specializing in Feng Shui, Mian Xiang (Face Reading) and BaZi (Destiny Analysis) consulting services worldwide. Joey Yap - an internationally renowned Master Trainer, Consultant, Speaker and best-selling Author - has dedicated his life to the art and science of Chinese Metaphysics.

JYCG has its main office in Kuala Lumpur, and draws upon its diverse reservoir of strength from a group of dedicated and experienced consultants based in more than 30 countries, worldwide.

As the pioneer in blending established, classical Chinese Metaphysics techniques with the latest approach in consultation practices, JYCG has built its reputation on the principles of professionalism and only the highest standards of service. This allows us to retain the cutting edge in delivering Feng Shui and Destiny consultation services to both corporate and personal clients, in a simple and direct manner, without compromising on quality.

Across Industries: Our Portfolio of Clients

Our diverse portfolio of both corporate and individual clients from all around the world bears testimony to our experience and capabilities.

Virtually every industry imaginable has benefited from our services - ranging from academic and financial institutions, real-estate developers and multinational corporations, to those in the leisure and tourism industry. Our services are also engaged by professionals, prominent business personalities, celebrities, high-profile politicians and people from all walks of life.

JOEY YAP CONSULTING GROUP

Name (Mr./Mrs./Ms.):_____

Contact Details

Tel:_____ Fax:_____

Mobile :_____

E-mail:_____

What Type of Consultation Are You Interested In?
☐ Feng Shui ☐ BaZi ☐ Date Selection ☐ Yi Jing

Please tick if applicable:
☐ Are you a Property Developer looking to engage Joey Yap Consulting Group?

☐ Are you a Property Investor looking for tailor-made packages to suit your investment requirements?

Please attach your name card here.

Thank you for completing this form. Please fax it back to us at:

Malaysia & the rest of the world
Fax : +603-2284 2213   Tel : +603-2284 1213

www.joeyyap.com

Feng Shui Consultations

For Residential Properties
• Initial Land/Property Assessment
• Residential Feng Shui Consultations
• Residential Land Selection
• End-to-End Residential Consultation

For Commercial Properties
• Initial Land/Property Assessment
• Commercial Feng Shui Consultations
• Commercial Land Selection
• End-to-End Commercial Consultation

For Property Developers
• End-to-End Consultation
• Post-Consultation Advisory Services
• Panel Feng Shui Consultant

For Property Investors
• Your Personal Feng Shui Consultant
• Tailor-Made Packages

For Memorial Parks & Burial Sites
• Yin House Feng Shui

BaZi Consultations

Personal Destiny Analysis
• Personal Destiny Analysis for Individuals
• Children's BaZi Analysis
• Family BaZi Analysis

Strategic Analysis for Corporate Organizations
• Corporate BaZi Consultations
• BaZi Analysis for Human Resource Management

Entrepreneurs & Business Owners
• BaZi Analysis for Entrepreneurs

Career Pursuits
• BaZi Career Analysis

Relationships
• Marriage and Compatibility Analysis
• Partnership Analysis

For Everyone
• Annual BaZi Forecast
• Your Personal BaZi Coach

Date Selection Consultations

• **Marriage Date Selection**
• **Caesarean Birth Date Selection**
• **House-Moving Date Selection**
• **Renovation & Groundbreaking Dates**

• **Signing of Contracts**
• **Official Openings**
• **Product Launches**

Yi Jing Assessment

A Time-Tested, Accurate Science

• With a history predating 4 millennia, the Yi Jing - or Classic of Change - is one of the oldest Chinese texts surviving today. Its purpose as an oracle, in predicting the outcome of things, is based on the variables of Time, Space and Specific Events.

• A Yi Jing Assessment provides specific answers to any specific questions you may have about a specific event or endeavor. This is something that a Destiny Analysis would not be able to give you.

Basically, what a Yi Jing Assessment does is focus on only ONE aspect or item at a particular point in your life, and give you a calculated prediction of the details that will follow suit, if you undertake a particular action. It gives you an insight into a situation, and what course of action to take in order to arrive at a satisfactory outcome at the end of the day.

Please Contact JYCG for a personalized Yi Jing Assessment!

INVITING US TO YOUR CORPORATE EVENTS

Many reputable organizations and institutions have worked closely with JYCG to build a synergistic business relationship by engaging our team of consultants, led by Joey Yap, as speakers at their corporate events. Our seminars and short talks are always packed with audiences consisting of clients and associates of multinational and public-listed companies as well as key stakeholders of financial institutions.

We tailor our seminars and talks to suit the anticipated or pertinent group of audience. Be it a department, subsidiary, your clients or even the entire corporation, we aim to fit your requirements in delivering the intended message(s).

CHINESE METAPHYSICS REFERENCE SERIES

The Chinese Metaphysics Reference Series is a collection of reference texts, source material, and educational textbooks to be used as supplementary guides by scholars, students, researchers, teachers and practitioners of Chinese Metaphysics.

These comprehensive and structured books provide fast, easy reference to aid in the study and practice of various Chinese Metaphysics subjects including Feng Shui, BaZi, Yi Jing, Zi Wei, Liu Ren, Ze Ri, Ta Yi, Qi Men and Mian Xiang.

The Chinese Metaphysics Compendium

At over 1,000 pages, the *Chinese Metaphysics Compendium* is a unique one-volume reference book that compiles all the formulas relating to Feng Shui, BaZi (Four Pillars of Destiny), Zi Wei (Purple Star Astrology), Yi Jing (I-Ching), Qi Men (Mystical Doorways), Ze Ri (Date Selection), Mian Xiang (Face Reading) and other sources of Chinese Metaphysics.

It is presented in the form of easy-to-read tables, diagrams and reference charts, all of which are compiled into one handy book. This first-of-its-kind compendium is presented in both English and the original Chinese, so that none of the meanings and contexts of the technical terminologies are lost.

The only essential and comprehensive reference on Chinese Metaphysics, and an absolute must-have for all students, scholars, and practitioners of Chinese Metaphysics.

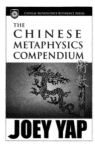

The Ten Thousand Year Calendar (Pocket Edition)	The Ten Thousand Year Calendar	Dong Gong Date Selection	The Date Selection Compendium	Plum Blossoms Divination Reference Book	San Yuan Dragon Gate Eight Formations Water Method	Xuan Kong Da Gua Ten Thousand Year Calendar
Bazi Hour Pillar Useful Gods - Wood	Bazi Hour Pillar Useful Gods - Fire	Bazi Hour Pillar Useful Gods - Earth	Bazi Hour Pillar Useful Gods - Metal	Bazi Hour Pillar Useful Gods - Water	Xuan Kong Da Gua Structures Reference Book	Xuan Kong Da Gua 64 Gua Transformation Analysis
						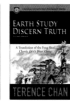
Bazi Structures and Structural Useful Gods - Wood	Bazi Structures and Structural Useful Gods - Fire	Bazi Structures and Structural Useful Gods - Earth	Bazi Structures and Structural Useful Gods - Metal	Bazi Structures and Structural Useful Gods - Water	Xuan Kong Purple White Script	Earth Study Discern Truth Second Edition

Educational Tools & Software

Xuan Kong Flying Stars Feng Shui Software
The Essential Application for Enthusiasts and Professionals

The Xuan Kong Flying Stars Feng Shui Software is a brand-new application by Joey Yap that will assist you in the practice of Xuan Kong Feng Shui with minimum fuss and maximum effectiveness. Superimpose the Flying Stars charts over your house plans (or those of your clients) to clearly demarcate the 9 Palaces. Use it to help you create fast and sophisticated chart drawings and presentations, as well as to assist professional practitioners in the report-writing process before presenting the final reports for your clients. Students can use it to practice their Xuan Kong Feng Shui skills and knowledge, and it can even be used by designers and architects!

Some of the highlights of the software include:
- Natal Flying Stars
- Monthly Flying Stars
- 81 Flying Stars Combinations
- Dual-View Format

- Annual Flying Stars
- Flying Stars Integration
- 24 Mountains

All charts will be are printable and configurable, and can be saved for future editing. Also, you'll be able to export your charts into most image file formats like jpeg, bmp, and gif.

The Xuan Kong Flying Stars Feng Shui Software can make your Feng Shui practice simpler and more effective, garnering you amazing results with less effort!

Mini Feng Shui Compass

This Mini Feng Shui Compass with the accompanying Companion Booklet written by leading Feng Shui and Chinese Astrology Master Trainer Joey Yap is a must-have for any Feng Shui enthusiast.

The Mini Feng Shui Compass is a self-aligning compass that is not only light at 100gms but also built sturdily to ensure it will be convenient to use anywhere. The rings on the Mini Feng Shui Compass are bi-lingual and incorporate the 24 Mountain Rings that is used in your traditional Luo Pan.

The comprehensive booklet included will guide you in applying the 24 Mountain Directions on your Mini Feng Shui Compass effectively and the 8 Mansions Feng Shui to locate the most auspicious locations within your home, office and surroundings. You can also use the Mini Feng Shui Compass when measuring the direction of your property for the purpose of applying Flying Stars Feng Shui.

Educational Tools & Software

BaZi Ming Pan Software Version 2.0
Professional Four Pillars Calculator for Destiny Analysis

The BaZi Ming Pan Version 2.0 Professional Four Pillars Calculator for Destiny Analysis is the most technically advanced software of its kind in the world today. It allows even those without any knowledge of BaZi to generate their own BaZi Charts, and provides virtually every detail required to undertake a comprehensive Destiny Analysis.

This Professional Four Pillars Calculator allows you to even undertake a day-to-day analysis of your Destiny. What's more, all BaZi Charts generated by this software are fully printable and configurable! Designed for both enthusiasts and professional practitioners, this state-of-the-art software blends details with simplicity, and is capable of generating 4 different types of BaZi charts: **BaZi Professional Charts, BaZi Annual Analysis Charts, BaZi Pillar Analysis Charts and BaZi Family Relationship Charts.**

Additional references, configurable to cater to all levels of BaZi knowledge and usage, include:
• Dual Age & Bilingual Option (Western & Chinese) • Na Yin narrations • 12 Life Stages evaluation • Death & Emptiness • Gods & Killings • Special Days • Heavenly Virtue Nobles

This software also comes with a Client Management feature that allows you to save and trace clients' records instantly, navigate effortlessly between BaZi charts, and file your clients' information in an organized manner.

The BaZi Ming Pan Version 2.0 Calculator sets a new standard by combining the best of BaZi and technology.

Joey Yap Feng Shui Template Set

Directions are the cornerstone of any successful Feng Shui audit or application. The **Joey Yap Feng Shui Template Set** is a set of three templates to simplify the process of taking directions and determining locations and positions, whether it's for a building, a house, or an open area such as a plot of land, all with just a floor plan or area map.

The Set comprises 3 basic templates: The Basic Feng Shui Template, 8 Mansions Feng Shui Template, and the Flying Stars Feng Shui Template.

With bi-lingual notations for these directions; both in English and the original Chinese, the **Joey Yap Feng Shui Template Set** comes with its own Booklet that gives simple yet detailed instructions on how to make use of the 3 templates within.

• Easy-to-use, simple, and straightforward
• Small and portable; each template measuring only 5" x 5"
• Additional 8 Mansions and Flying Stars Reference Rings
• Handy companion booklet with usage tips and examples

Accelerate Your Face Reading Skills With
Joey Yap's Face Reading Revealed DVD Series

Mian Xiang, the Chinese art of Face Reading, is an ancient form of physiognomy and entails the use of the face and facial characteristics to evaluate key aspects of a person's life, luck and destiny. In his Face Reading DVDs series, Joey Yap shows you how the facial features reveal a wealth of information about a person's luck, destiny and personality.

Mian Xiang also tell us the talents, quirks and personality of an individual. Do you know that just by looking at a person's face, you can ascertain his or her health, wealth, relationships and career? Let Joey Yap show you how the 12 Palaces can be utilised to reveal a person's inner talents, characteristics and much more.

Each facial feature on the face represents one year in a person's life. Your face is a 100-year map of your life and each position reveals your fortune and destiny at a particular age as well as insights and information about your personality, skills, abilities and destiny.

Using Mian Xiang, you will also be able to plan your life ahead by identifying, for example, the right business partner and knowing the sort of person that you need to avoid. By knowing their characteristics through the facial features, you will be able to gauge their intentions and gain an upper hand in negotiations.

Do you know what moles signify? Do they bring good or bad luck? Do you want to build better relationships with your partner or family members or have your ever wondered why you seem to be always bogged down by trivial problems in your life?

In these highly entertaining DVDs, Joey will help you answer all these questions and more. You will be able to ascertain the underlying meaning of moles, birthmarks or even the type of your hair in Face Reading. Joey will also reveal the guidelines to help you foster better and stronger relationships with your loved ones through Mian Xiang.

Feng Shui for Homebuyers DVD Series

Best-selling Author, and international Master Trainer and Consultant Joey Yap reveals in these DVDs the significant Feng Shui features that every homebuyer should know when evaluating a property.

Joey will guide you on how to customise your home to maximise the Feng Shui potential of your property and gain the full benefit of improving your health, wealth and love life using the 9 Palace Grid. He will show you how to go about applying the classical applications of the Life Gua and House Gua techniques to get attuned to your Sheng Qi (positive energies).

In these DVDs, you will also learn how to identify properties with good Feng Shui features that will help you promote a fulfilling life and achieve your full potential. Discover how to avoid properties with negative Feng Shui that can bring about detrimental effects to your health, wealth and relationships.

Joey will also elaborate on how to fix the various aspects of your home that may have an impact on the Feng Shui of your property and give pointers on how to tap into the positive energies to support your goals.

Discover Feng Shui with Joey Yap (TV Series)

Discover Feng Shui with Joey Yap: Set of 4 DVDs

Informative and entertaining, classical Feng Shui comes alive in *Discover Feng Shui with Joey Yap!*

Dying to know how you can use Feng Shui to improve your house or office, but simply too busy attend for formal classes?

You have the questions. Now let Joey personally answer them in this 4-set DVD compilation! Learn how to ensure the viability of your residence or workplace, Feng Shui-wise, without having to convert it into a Chinese antiques' shop. Classical Feng Shui is about harnessing the natural power of your environment to improve quality of life. It's a systematic and subtle metaphysical science.

And that's not all. Joey also debunks many a myth about classical Feng Shui, and shares with viewers Face Reading tips as well!

Own the series that national channel 8TV did a re-run of in 2005, today!

Continue Your Journey with Joey Yap's Books

Mian Xiang - Discover Face Reading (English & Chinese versions)

Need to identify a suitable business partner? How about understanding your staff or superiors better? Or even choosing a suitable spouse? These mind boggling questions can be answered in Joey Yap's introductory book to Face Reading titled *Mian Xiang – Discover Face Reading*. This book will help you discover the hidden secrets in a person's face.

Mian Xiang – Discover Face Reading is comprehensive book on all areas of Face Reading, covering some of the most important facial features, including the forehead, mouth, ears and even the philtrum above your lips. This book will help you analyse not just your Destiny but help you achieve your full potential and achieve life fulfillment.

Joey Yap's Art of Face Reading

The Art of Face Reading is Joey Yap's second effort with CICO Books, and takes a lighter, more practical approach to Face Reading. This book does not so much focus on the individual features as it does on reading the entire face. It is about identifying common personality types and characters.

Joey shows readers how to identify successful career faces, or faces that are most likely to be able to do well financially. He also explores Face Reading in the context of health. He uses examples of real people - famous and ordinary folk - to allow readers to better understand what these facial features look like on an actual face. Readers will learn how to identify faces in Career, Wealth, Relationships, and Health (eg. 'The Salesperson Face,' 'The Politician Face,' 'The Unfaithful One,' 'The Shopaholic One,' and plenty more.)

Easy Guide on Face Reading (English & Chinese versions)

The Face Reading Essentials series of books comprise 5 individual books on the key features of the fac Eyes, Eyebrows, Ears, Nose, and Mouth. Each book provides a detailed illustration and a simple yet descrip explanation on the individual types of the features.

The books are equally useful and effective for beginners, enthusiasts, and the curious. The series is designe enable people who are new to Face Reading to make the most of first impressions and learn to apply Face Reac skills to understand the personality and character of friends, family, co-workers, and even business associate

 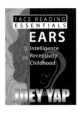 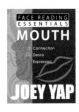 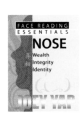 

Continue Your Journey with Joey Yap's Books

Three Levels of BaZi Profiling (English & Chinese versions)

In BaZi Profiling, there are three levels that reflect three different stages of a person's personal nature and character structure.

Level 1 – The Day Master

The Day Master in a nutshell is the BASIC YOU. The inborn personality. It is your essential character. It answers the basic question "WHO AM I". There are ten basic personality profiles – the TEN Day Masters – each with its unique set of personality traits, likes and dislikes.

Level 2 – The Structure

The Structure is your behavior and attitude – in other words, how you use your personality. It expands on the Day Master (Level 1). The structure reveals your natural tendencies in life – are you more controlling, more of a creator, supporter, thinker or connector? Each of the Ten Day Masters express themselves differently through the FIVE Structures. Why do we do the things we do? Why do we like the things we like? – The answers are in our BaZi STRUCTURE.

Level 3 – The Profile

The Profile reveals your unique abilities and skills, the masks that you consciously and unconsciously "put on" as you approach and navigate the world. Your Profile speaks of your ROLES in life. There are TEN roles – or Ten BaZi Profiles. Everyone plays a different role.

What makes you happy and what does success mean to you is different to somebody else. Your sense of achievement and sense of purpose in life is unique to your Profile. Your Profile will reveal your unique style.

The path of least resistance to your success and wealth can only be accessed once you get into your "flow." Your BaZi Profile reveals how you can get FLOW. It will show you your patterns in work, relationship and social settings. Being AWARE of these patterns is your first step to positive Life Transformation.

Continue Your Journey with Joey Yap's Books

Walking the Dragons

Walking the Dragons is a guided tour through the classical landform Feng Shui of ancient China, an enchanting collection of deeply-researched yet entertaining essays rich in historical detail.

Compiled in one book for the first time from Joey Yap's Feng Shui Mastery Excursion Series, the book highlights China's extensive, vibrant history with astute observations on the Feng Shui of important sites and places. Learn the landform formations of Yin Houses (tombs and burial places), as well as mountains, temples, castles, and villages.

It demonstrates complex Feng Shui theories and principles in easy-to-understand, entertaining language and is the perfect addition to the bookshelf of a Feng Shui or history lover. Anyone, whether experienced in Feng Shui or new to the practice, will be able to enjoy the insights shared in this book. Complete with gorgeous full-colour pictures of all the amazing sights and scenery, it's the next best thing to having been there yourself!

Your Aquarium Here

Your Aquarium Here is a simple, practical, hands-on Feng Shui book that teaches you how to incorporate a Water feature – an aquarium – for optimal Feng Shui benefit, whether for personal relationships, wealth, or career. Designed to be comprehensive yet simple enough for a novice or beginner, *Your Aquarium Here* provides historical and factual information about the role of Water in Feng Shui, and provides a step-by-step guide to installing and using an aquarium.

The book is the first in the **Fengshuilogy Series**, a series of matter-of-fact and useful Feng Shui books designed for the person who wants to do fuss-free Feng Shui. Not everyone who wants to use Feng Shui is an expert or a scholar! This series of books are just the kind you'd want on your bookshelf to gain basic, practical knowledge of the subject. Go ahead and Feng Shui-It-Yourself – *Your Aquarium Here* eliminates all the fuss and bother, but maintains all the fun and excitement, of authentic Feng Shui application!

The Art of Date Selection: Personal Date Selection

In today's modern world, it is not good enough to just do things effectively – we need to do them efficiently, as well. From the signing of business contracts and moving into a new home, to launching a product or even tying the knot; everything has to move, and move very quickly too. There is a premium on Time, where mistakes can indeed be costly.

The notion of doing the Right Thing, at the Right Time and in the Right Place is the very backbone of Date Selection. Because by selecting a suitable date specially tailored to a specific activity or endeavor, we infuse it with the most positive energies prevalent in our environment during that particular point in time; and that could well make the difference between `make-and-break'! With the *Art of Date Selection: Personal Date Selection*, learn simple, practical methods you can employ to select not just good dates, but personalized good dates. Whether it's a personal activity such as a marriage or professional endeavor such as launching a business, signing a contract or even acquiring assets, this book will show you how to pick the good dates and tailor them to suit the activity in question, as well as avoid the negative ones too!

Pure Feng Shui

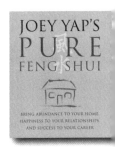

Pure Feng Shui is Joey Yap's debut with an international publisher, CICO Books, and is a refreshing and elegant look at the intricacies of Classical Feng Shui – now compiled in a useful manner for modern-day readers. This book is a comprehensive introduction to all the important precepts and techniques of Feng Shui practice.

He reveals how to use Feng Shui to bring prosperity, good relationships, and success into one's life the simple and genuine way – without having to resort to symbols or figurines! He shows readers how to work with what they have and make simple and sustainable changes that can have significant Feng Shui effect. The principles of Classical Feng Shui and Chinese Astrology inform his teachings and explanations, so all that the readers need are a compass, a pencil, some paper, and an open mind!

Continue Your Journey with Joey Yap's Books

Feng Shui For Homebuyers - Exterior (English & Chinese versions)

Best selling Author and international Feng Shui Consultant, Joey Yap, will guide you on the various important features in your external environment that have a bearing on the Feng Shui of your home. For homeowners, those looking to build their own home or even investors who are looking to apply Feng Shui to their homes, this book provides valuable information from the classical Feng Shui theories and applications.

This book will assist you in screening and eliminating unsuitable options with negative FSQ (Feng Shui Quotient) should you acquire your own land or if you are purchasing a newly built home. It will also help you in determining which plot of land to select and which to avoid when purchasing an empty parcel of land.

Feng Shui for Homebuyers - Interior (English & Chinese versions)

A book every homeowner or potential house buyer should have. The Feng Shui for Homebuyers (Interior) is an informative reference book and invaluable guide written by best selling Author and international Feng Shui Consultant, Joey Yap.

This book provides answers to the important questions of what really does matter when looking at the internal Feng Shui of a home or office. It teaches you how to analyze your home or office floor plans and how to improve their Feng Shui. It will answer all your questions about the positive and negative flow of Qi within your home and ways to utilize them to your maximum benefit.

Providing you with a guide to calculating your Life Gua and House Gua to fine-tune your Feng Shui within your property, Joey Yap focuses on practical, easily applicable ideas on what you can implement internally in a property.

Feng Shui for Apartment Buyers - Home Owners

Finding a good apartment or condominium is never an easy task but who do you ensure that is also has good Feng Shui? And how exactly do you apply Feng Shui to an apartment or condominium or high-rise residence?

These questions and more are answered by renowned Feng Shui Consultant and Master Trainer Joey Yap in **Feng Shui for Apartment Buyers - Home Owners**. Joey answers the key questions about Feng Shui and apartments, then guides you through the bare basics like taking a direction and super-imposing a Flying Stars chart onto a floor plan. Joey also walks you through the process of finding an apartment with favorable Feng Shui, sharing with you some of the key methods and techniques that are employed by professional Feng Shui consultants in assesing apartment Feng Shui.

In his trademark straight-to-the-point manner, Joey shares with you the Feng Shui do's and dont's when it comes to finding an apartment with favorable Feng Shui and which is conducive for home living.

Continue Your Journey with Joey Yap's Books

Stories and Lessons on Feng Shui (English & Chinese versions)

Stories and Lessons on Feng Shui is a compilation of essays and stories written by leading Feng Shui and Chinese Astrology trainer and consultant Joey Yap about Feng Shui and Chinese Astrology.

In this heart-warming collection of easy to read stories, find out why it's a myth that you should never have Water on the right hand side of your house, the truth behind the infamous 'love' and 'wealth' corners and that the sudden death of a pet fish is really NOT due to bad luck!

More Stories and Lessons on Feng Shui

Finally, the long-awaited sequel to *Stories & Lessons on Feng Shui*!

If you've read the best-selling Stories & Lessons on Feng Shui, you won't want to miss this book. And even if you haven't read *Stories & Lessons on Feng Shui*, there's always a time to rev your Feng Shui engine up.

The time is NOW.

And the book? *More Stories & Lessons on Feng Shui* – the 2nd compilation of the most popular articles and columns penned by Joey Yap; **specially featured in national and international publications, magazines and newspapers.**

All in all, *More Stories & Lessons on Feng Shui* is a delightful chronicle of Joey's articles, thoughts and vast experience - as a professional Feng Shui consultant and instructor - that have been purposely refined, edited and expanded upon to make for a light-hearted, interesting yet educational read. And with Feng Shui, BaZi, Mian Xiang and Yi Jing all thrown into this one dish, there's something for everyone...so all you need to serve or accompany *More Stories & Lessons on Feng Shui* with is your favorite cup of tea or coffee!

Even More Stories and Lessons on Feng Shui

In this third release in the Stories and Lessons series, Joey Yap continues his exploration on the study and practice of Feng Shui in the modern age through a series of essays and personal anecdotes. Debunking superstition, offering simple and understandable "Feng Shui-It-Yourself" tips, and expounding on the history and origins of classical Feng Shui, Joey takes readers on a journey that is always refreshing and exciting.

Besides 'behind-the-scenes' revelations of actual Feng Shui audits, there are also chapters on how beginners can easily and accurately incorporate Feng Shui practice into their lives, as well as travel articles that offer proof that when it comes to Feng Shui, the Qi literally knows no boundaries.

In his trademark lucid and forthright style, Joey covers themes and topics that will strike a chord with all readers who have an interest in Feng Shui.

Xuan Kong: Flying Stars Feng Shui

Xuan Kong Flying Stars Feng Shui is an essential introductory book to the subject of Xuan Kong Fei Xing, a well-known and popular system of Feng Shui, written by International Feng Shui Master Trainer Joey Yap.

In his down-to-earth, entertaining and easy to read style, Joey Yap takes you through the essential basics of Classical Feng Shui, and the key concepts of Xuan Kong Fei Xing (Flying Stars). Learn how to fly the stars, plot a Flying Star chart for your home or office and interpret the stars and star combinations. Find out how to utilise the favourable areas of your home or office for maximum benefit and learn 'tricks of the trade' and 'trade secrets' used by Feng Shui practitioners to enhance and maximise Qi in your home or office.

An essential integral introduction to the subject of Classical Feng Shui and the Flying Stars System of Feng Shui!

Continue Your Journey with Joey Yap's Books

BaZi - The Destiny Code (English & Chinese versions)

Leading Chinese Astrology Master Trainer Joey Yap makes it easy to learn how to unlock your Destiny through your BaZi with this book. BaZi or Four Pillars of Destiny is an ancient Chinese science which enables individuals to understand their personality, hidden talents and abilities as well as their luck cycle, simply by examining the information contained within their birth data. *The Destiny Code* is the first book that shows readers how to plot and interpret their own Destiny Charts and lays the foundation for more in-depth BaZi studies. Written in a lively entertaining style, the Destiny Code makes BaZi accessible to the layperson. Within 10 chapters, understand and appreciate more about this astoundingly accurate ancient Chinese Metaphysical science.

BaZi - The Destiny Code Revealed (English & Chinese versions)

In this follow up to Joey Yap's best-selling *The Destiny Code*, delve deeper into your own Destiny chart through an understanding of the key elemental relationships that affect the Heavenly Stems and Earthly Branches. Find out how Combinations, Clash, Harm, Destructions and Punishments bring new dimension to a BaZi chart. Complemented by extensive real-life examples, *The Destiny Code Revealed* takes you to the next level of BaZi, showing you how to unlock the Codes of Destiny and to take decisive action at the right time, and capitalise on the opportunities in life.

The Ten Gods
An Introduction to The Ten Gods in BaZi

The Ten Gods, being an integral and core component of the study of BaZi (Chinese Astrology), are the key to Decoding the Destiny Code. Anyone who wishes to make use of BaZi must have a strong foundation in the Ten Gods.

The Ten Gods represent every conceivable aspect, object and item in life, both the tangible and the intangible. As such, a person's life, in every sense of the word, is ultimately defined by the Ten Gods present (and absent) in a BaZi chart.

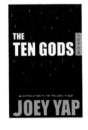

Knowing how to identify the Ten Gods of each of the Ten Day Masters, and understanding the basic fundamentals of each of the Ten Gods is a breakthrough step in analyzing and accurately deriving information about a person, be it their character, or their destiny, from their BaZi chart.

This book presents a one-of-a-kind reference designed to provide a thorough introduction to the specific subject matter, the Ten Gods in BaZi.

It provides readers with a 360-degree perspective - a well-rounded standpoint - on the subject, covering the discussion about each of the Ten Gods written to include both the traditional, orthodox and conventional perspective, and the modern, less traditional perspective, along with the pros and cons of each of the Ten Gods attributes. It also demonstrates simple but useful methods of analyzing a BaZi chart using the Ten Gods.

Annual Releases

Chinese Astrology for 2011

This information-packed annual guide to the Chinese Astrology for 2011 goes way beyond the conventional 'animal horoscope' book. To begin with, author Joey Yap includes a personalized outlook for 2011 based on the individual's BaZi Day Pillar (Jia Zi) and a 12-month micro-analysis for each of the 60 Day Pillars – in addition to the annual outlook for all 12 animal signs and the 12-month outlook for each animal sign in 2011. Find out what awaits you in 2011 from the four key aspects of Health, Wealth, Career and Relationships…with Joey Yap's **Chinese Astrology for 2011**!

Feng Shui for 2011

Maximize the Qi of the Year of the Metal Tiger for your home and office, with Joey Yap's **Feng Shui for 2011** book. Learn how to tap into the positive sectors of the year, and avoid the negative ones and those with the Annual Afflictions, as well as ascertain how the annual Flying Stars affect your property by comparing them against the Eight Mansions (Ba Zhai) for 2011. Flying Stars enthusiasts will also find this book handy, as it includes the monthly Flying Stars charts for the year, accompanied by detailed commentaries on what sectors to use and avoid – to enable you to optimize your Academic, Relationships and Wealth Luck in 2011.

Pro Tong Shu Diary 2011

An ideal Tong Shu tool for professionals and experienced Feng Shui practitioners, the Professional Edition is designed to fulfill the requirements of those who need to perform Date Selection on a regular or specialised basis. This handy edition eliminates the need to search through many references when all the required information to select a good date is contained within this volume.

The Professional Edition comes in an elegant cover - a must-have whether you're a practitioner, student or simply a keen enthusiast.

Tong Shu Diary 2011

Enhance and organize your career and personal paths with Tong Shu Diary 2011. It will serve as your professional organizer, with a twist: You will hold the higher ground in determining the suitability of dates for your entire year's activities! This holistic Diary fuses the elements of the Chinese Solar and Lunar Calendars, with the lingua france of the Gregorian Calendar.

Weekly Tong Shu Diary 2011

Organize your professional and personal lives with the **Tong Shu Diary 2011**, with a twist… it also allows you to determine the most suitable dates on which you can undertake important activities and endeavors throughout the year! This compact Diary integrates the Chinese Solar and Lunar Calendars with the universal lingua franca of the Gregorian Calendar.

Tong Shu Monthly Planner 2011

Tailor-made for the Feng Shui or BaZi enthusiast in you, or even professional Chinese Metaphysics consultants who want a compact planner with useful information incorporated into it. In the **Tong Shu Monthly Planner 2011**, you will find the auspicious and inauspicious dates for the year marked out for you, alongside the most suitable activities to be undertaken on each day. As a bonus, there is also a reference section containing all the monthly Flying Stars charts and Annual Afflictions for 2011.

Tong Shu Desktop Calendar 2011

Get an instant snapshot of the suitable and unsuitable activities for each day of the Year of the Earth Rat, with the icons displayed on this lightweight Desktop Calendar. Elegantly presenting the details of the Chinese Solar Calendar in the form of the standard Gregorian one, the **Tong Shu Desktop Calendar 2011** is perfect for Chinese Metaphysics enthusiasts and practitioners alike. Whether it a business launching or meeting, ground breaking ceremony, travel or house-moving that you have in mind, this Calendar is designed to fulfill your information needs.

Elevate Your Feng Shui Skills With Joey Yap's Home Study Course And Educational DVDs

Xuan Kong Vol.1
An Advanced Feng Shui Home Study Course

Learn the Xuan Kong Flying Star Feng Shui system in just 20 lessons! Joey Yap's specialised notes and course work have been written to enable distance learning without compromising on the breadth or quality of the syllabus. Learn at your own pace with the same material students in a live class would use. The most comprehensive distance learning course on Xuan Kong Flying Star Feng Shui in the market. Xuan Kong Flying Star Vol.1 comes complete with a special binder for all your course notes.

Feng Shui for Period 8 - (DVD)

Don't miss the Feng Shui Event of the next 20 years! Catch Joey Yap LIVE and find out just what Period 8 is all about. This DVD boxed set zips you through the fundamentals of Feng Shui and the impact of this important change in the Feng Shui calendar. Joey's entertaining, conversational style walks you through the key changes that Period 8 will bring and how to tap into Wealth Qi and Good Feng Shui for the next 20 years.

Xuan Kong Flying Stars Beginners Workshop - (DVD)

Take a front row seat in Joey Yap's Xuan Kong Flying Stars workshop with this unique LIVE RECORDING of Joey Yap's Xuan Kong Flying Stars Feng Shui workshop, attended by over 500 people. This DVD program provides an effective and quick introduction of Xuan Kong Feng Shui essentials for those who are just starting out in their study of classical Feng Shui. Learn to plot your own Flying Star chart in just 3 hours. Learn 'trade secret' methods, remedies and cures for Flying Stars Feng Shui. This boxed set contains 3 DVDs and 1 workbook with notes and charts for reference.

BaZi Four Pillars of Destiny Beginners Workshop - (DVD)

Ever wondered what Destiny has in store for you? Or curious to know how you can learn more about your personality and inner talents? BaZi or Four Pillars of Destiny is an ancient Chinese science that enables us to understand a person's hidden talent, inner potential, personality, health and wealth luck from just their birth data. This specially compiled DVD set of Joey Yap's BaZi Beginners Workshop provides a thorough and comprehensive introduction to BaZi. Learn how to read your own chart and understand your own luck cycle. This boxed set contains 3 DVDs and 1 workbook with notes and reference charts.

Interested in learning MORE about Feng Shui? Advance Your Feng Shui Knowledge with the Mastery Academy Courses.

Feng Shui Mastery Series™
LIVE COURSES (MODULES ONE TO FOUR)

Feng Shui Mastery – Module One
Beginners Course

Designed for students seeking an entry-level intensive program into the study of Feng Shui , Module One is an intensive foundation course that aims not only to provide you with an introduction to Feng Shui theories and formulas and equip you with the skills and judgments to begin practicing and conduct simple Feng Shui audits upon successful completion of the course. Learn all about Forms, Eight Mansions Feng Shui and Flying Star Feng Shui in just one day with a unique, structured learning program that makes learning Feng Shui quick and easy!

Feng Shui Mastery – Module Two
Practitioners Course

Building on the knowledge and foundation in classical Feng Shui theory garnered in M1, M2 provides a more advanced and in-depth understanding of Eight Mansions, Xuan Kong Flying Star and San He and introduces students to theories that are found only in the classical Chinese Feng Shui texts. This 3-Day Intensive course hones analytical and judgment skills, refines Luo Pan (Chinese Feng Shui compass) skills and reveals 'trade secret' remedies. Module Two covers advanced Forms Analysis, San He's Five Ghost Carry Treasure formula, Advanced Eight Mansions and Xuan Kong Flying Stars and equips you with the skills needed to undertake audits and consultations for residences and offices.

Feng Shui Mastery – Module Three
Advanced Practitioners Course

Module Three is designed for Professional Feng Shui Practitioners. Learn advanced topics in Feng Shui and take your skills to a cutting edge level. Be equipped with the knowledge, techniques and confidence to conduct large scale audits (like estate and resort planning). Learn how to apply different systems appropriately to remedy situations or cases deemed inauspicious by one system and reconcile conflicts in different systems of Feng Shui. Gain advanced knowledge of San He (Three Harmony) systems and San Yuan (Three Cycles) systems, advanced Luan Tou (Forms Feng Shui) and specialist Water Formulas.

Feng Shui Mastery – Module Four
Master Course

The graduating course of the Feng Shui Mastery (FSM) Series, this course takes the advanced practitioner to the Master level. Power packed M4 trains students to 'walk the mountains' and identify superior landform, superior grade structures and make qualitative evaluations of landform, structures, Water and Qi and covers advanced and exclusive topics of San He, San Yuan, Xuan Kong, Ba Zhai, Luan Tou (Advanced Forms and Water Formula) Feng Shui. Master Internal, External and Luan Tou (Landform) Feng Shui methodologies to apply Feng Shui at every level and undertake consultations of every scale and magnitude, from houses and apartments to housing estates, townships, shopping malls and commercial districts.

BaZi Mastery – Module One
Intensive Foundation Course

This Intensive One Day Foundation Course provides an introduction to the principles and fundamentals of BaZi (Four Pillars of Destiny) and Destiny Analysis methods such as Ten Gods, Useful God and Strength of Qi. Learn how to plot a BaZi chart and interpret your Destiny and your potential. Master BaZi and learn to capitalize on your strengths, minimize risks and downturns and take charge of your Destiny.

BaZi Mastery – Module Two
Practitioners Course

BaZi Module Two teaches students advanced BaZi analysis techniques and specific analysis methods for relationship luck, health evaluation, wealth potential and career potential. Students will learn to identify BaZi chart structures, sophisticated methods for applying the Ten Gods, and how to read Auxiliary Stars. Students who have completed Module Two will be able to conduct professional BaZi readings.

BaZi Mastery – Module Three
Advanced Practitioners Course

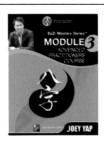

Designed for the BaZi practitioner, learn how to read complex cases and unique events in BaZi charts and perform Big and Small assessments. Discover how to analyze personalities and evaluate talents precisely, as well as special formulas and classical methodologies for BaZi from classics such as Di Tian Sui and Qiong Tong Bao Jian.

BaZi Mastery – Module Four
Master Course in BaZi

The graduating course of the BaZi Mastery Series, this course takes the advanced practitioner to the Masters' level. BaZi M4 focuses on specialized techniques of BaZi reading, unique special structures and advance methods from ancient classical texts. This program includes techniques on date selection and ancient methodologies from the Qiong Tong Bao Jian and Yuan Hai Zi Ping classics.

Xuan Kong Mastery – Module One
Advanced Foundation Course

This course is for the experienced Feng Shui professionals who wish to expand their knowledge and skills in the Xuan Kong system of Feng Shui, covering important foundation methods and techniques from the Wu Chang and Guang Dong lineages of Xuan Kong Feng Shui.

Xuan Kong Mastery – Module Two A
Advanced Xuan Kong Methodologies

Designed for Feng Shui practitioners seeking to specialise in the Xuan Kong system, this program focuses on methods of application and Joey Yap's unique Life Palace and Shifting Palace Methods, as well as methods and techniques from the Wu Chang lineage.

Xuan Kong Mastery – Module Two B
Purple White

Explore in detail and in great depth the star combinations in Xuan Kong. Learn how each different combination reacts or responds in different palaces, under different environmental circumstances and to whom in the property. Learn methods, theories and techniques extracted from ancient classics such as Xuan Kong Mi Zhi, Xuan Kong Fu, Fei Xing Fu and Zi Bai Jue.

Xuan Kong Mastery – Module Three
Advanced Xuan Kong Da Gua

This intensive course focuses solely on the Xuan Kong Da Gua system covering the theories, techniques and methods of application of this unique 64-Hexagram based system of Xuan Kong including Xuan Kong Da Gua for landform analysis.

Mian Xiang Mastery Series™
LIVE COURSES (MODULES ONE AND TWO)

Mian Xiang Mastery – Module One
Basic Face Reading

A person's face is their fortune – learn more about the ancient Chinese art of Face Reading. In just one day, be equipped with techniques and skills to read a person's face and ascertain their character, luck, wealth and relationship luck.

Mian Xiang Mastery – Module Two
Practical Face Reading

Mian Xiang Module Two covers face reading techniques extracted from the ancient classics Shen Xiang Quan Pian and Shen Xiang Tie Guan Dau. Gain a greater depth and understanding of Mian Xiang and learn to recognize key structures and characteristics in a person's face.

Yi Jing Mastery Series™
LIVE COURSES (MODULES ONE AND TWO)

Yi Jing Mastery – Module One
Traditional Yi Jing

'Yi', relates to change. Change is the only constant in life and the universe, without exception to this rule. The Yi Jing is hence popularly referred to as the Book or Classic of Change. Discoursed in the language of Yin and Yang, the Yi Jing is one of the oldest Chinese classical texts surviving today. With Traditional Yi Jing, learnn how this Classic is used to divine the outcomes of virtually every facet of life; from your relationships to seeking an answer to the issues you may face in your daily life.

Yi Jing Mastery – Module Two
Plum Blossom Numerology

Shao Yong, widely regarded as one of the greatest scholars of the Sung Dynasty, developed Mei Hua Yi Shu (Plum Blossom Numerology) as a more advanced means for divination purpose using the Yi Jing. In Plum Blossom Numerology, the results of a hexagram are interpreted by referring to the Gua meanings, where the interaction and relationship between the five elements, stems, branches and time are equally taken into consideration. This divination method, properly applied, allows us to make proper decisions whenever we find ourselves in a predicament.

Ze Ri Mastery Series™
LIVE COURSES (MODULES ONE AND TWO)

Ze Ri Mastery Series Module 1
Personal and Feng Shui Date Selection

The Mastery Academy's Date Selection Mastery Series Module 1 is specifically structured to provide novice students with an exciting introduction to the Art of Date Selection. Learn the rudiments and tenets of this intriguing metaphysical science. What makes a good date, and what makes a bad date? What dates are suitable for which activities, and what dates simply aren't? And of course, the mother of all questions: WHY aren't all dates created equal. All in only one Module – Module 1!

Ze Ri Mastery Series Module 2
Xuan Kong Da Gua Date Selection

In Module 2, discover advanced Date Selection techniques that will take your knowledge of this Art to a level equivalent to that of a professional's! This is the Module where Date Selection infuses knowledge of the ancient metaphysical science of Feng Shui and BaZi (Chinese Astrology, or Four Pillars of Destiny). Feng Shui, as a means of maximizing Human Luck (i.e. our luck on Earth), is often quoted as the cure to BaZi, which allows us to decipher our Heaven (i.e. inherent) Luck. And one of the most potent ways of making the most of what life has to offer us is to understand our Destiny, know how we can use the natural energies of our environment for our environments and MOST importantly, WHEN we should use these energies and for WHAT endeavors!

You will learn specific methods on how to select suitable dates, tailored to specific activities and events. More importantly, you will also be taught how to suit dates to a person's BaZi (Chinese Astrology, or Four Pillars of Destiny), in order to maximize his or her strengths, and allow this person to surmount any challenges that lie in wait. Add in the factor of `place', and you would have satisfied the notion of `doing the right thing, at the right time and in the right place'! A basic knowledge of BaZi and Feng Shui will come in handy in this Module, although these are not pre-requisites to successfully undergo Module 2.

Walk the Mountains! Learn Feng Shui in a Practical and Hands-on Program

 ## Feng Shui Mastery Excursion Series™: CHINA

Learn landform (Luan Tou) Feng Shui by walking the mountains and chasing the Dragon's vein in China. This Program takes the students in a study tour to examine notable Feng Shui landmarks, mountains, hills, valleys, ancient palaces, famous mansions, houses and tombs in China. The Excursion is a 'practical' hands-on course where students are shown to perform readings using the formulas they've learnt and to recognize and read Feng Shui Landform (Luan Tou) formations.

Read about China Excursion here:
http://www.masteryacademy.com/Education/schoolfengshui/fengshuimasteryexcursion.asp

Feng Shui for Life

Feng Shui for life is a 5-day course designed for the Feng Shui beginner to learn how to apply practical Feng Shui in day-to-day living. It is a culmination of powerful tools and techniques that allows you to gain quick proficiency in Classical Feng Shui. Discover quick tips on analysing your own BaZi, how to apply Feng Shui solutions for your own home, how to select auspicious dates for important activities, as well as simple and useful Face Reading techniques and practical Water Formulas. This is a complete beginner's course that is suitable for anyone with an interest in applying practical, real-world Feng Shui for life! Enhance every aspect of your life – your health, wealth, and relationships – using these easy-to-apply Classical Feng Shui methods.

Design Your Destiny

This is an introductory Program tailored for beginners on the study of BaZi. The Program teaches students the fundamentals of Personality Profiling and Destiny Analysis using BaZi, and guides them on plotting and reading the BaZi chart with confidence. This interactive workshop-style course encourages an enjoyable learning experience with proven fast results where students were able to apply what they've learnt instantly.

Mastery Academy courses are conducted around the world. Find out when will Joey Yap be in your area by visiting **www.masteryacademy.com** or call our office at **+603-2284 8080**.